HOARDS, HOUNDS AND HELMETS

The story of the Hallaton Treasure

Vicki Score

This book is dedicated to Ken and Hazel Wallace and the members
of the Hallaton Field Work Group

UNIVERSITY *of*
Leicester

Archaeological Services

University of Leicester Archaeological Services (ULAS) is a professional archaeological unit based in the School of Archaeology and Ancient History at the University of Leicester. ULAS undertakes archaeological projects all over the UK, mostly connected with planning applications for new developments, road schemes and quarries but also research excavations and community archaeology.

ULAS, School of Archaeology and Ancient History, University Road, Leicester LE1 7RH

Web: www.le.ac.uk/ulas   **Email: ulas@le.ac.uk**

The **School of Archaeology and Ancient History** at the University of Leicester can trace its origins back to 1958 and is now one of the foremost archaeology departments in the UK in terms of teaching, research and student satisfaction. Undergraduate and Postgraduate programmes are offered and the school also has a large and thriving Distance Learning community who study at Certificate, Undergraduate, Masters and PhD level. Staff have field projects all over the world, exploring the archaeologies of past societies from prehistoric through to early modern times. ULAS and the School run an annual training excavation, currently at the Iron Age hillfort of Burrough Hill in Leicestershire.

School of Archaeology and Ancient History, University Road, Leicester LE1 7RH

Web: www.le.ac.uk/departments/archaeology   **Email: arch-anchist@le.ac.uk**

Hallaton Field Work Group (HFWG) is a local community organisation set up to find out more about the heritage of east Leicestershire. This active group undertakes fieldwalking as well as geophysical survey using equipment purchased with a grant from the Lottery Heritage Fund. They also give local talks and training sessions and run annual excavations at Hallaton in conjunction with ULAS.

Email: hallatonfwg@yahoo.co.uk

Contents

Foreword

Every once in a while an archaeological discovery comes along that dramatically alters our understanding of a particular period of the past. The late Iron Age ritual focus at Hallaton is one such site. There can be little doubt that its investigation will rank among the most important archaeological projects carried out in Britain in the 21st century.

As this engaging account of the project by Vicki Score shows, the discoveries at Hallaton have added a completely new dimension to our understanding of Late Iron Age society and ritual on the eve of the Roman invasion. Detailed study of the many finds – from coins to animal bones – has provided new insights into the political and social organisation of the inhabitants of the region, as well as their beliefs and ritual practices. Above all, the results challenge conventional views of the extent of Roman influence and contacts with different British peoples in the period leading up to the Claudian invasion, strongly suggesting that the local elite was part of an international network that extended to the Mediterranean. Unlike peoples in other parts of Britain, it now looks as if they may well have welcomed the invaders. This in turn may explain why the settlement at Leicester, founded only fifty years earlier, was chosen by the Romans to be the administrative centre for the newly established *civitas* of the Corieltavi.

But the importance of Hallaton rests not only in the finds – extraordinary though they are. In an era when most excavations are undertaken by professional archaeologists working ahead of building development, this project is an outstanding example of what community archaeology can achieve, setting the standard for the integration of amateurs and professionals in a field project. From the moment of the discovery and reporting of the first coins by the Hallaton Field Work Group, through the investigation of the site in partnership with ULAS, careful study of the finds by a range of specialists at the University and the British Museum, and eventual acquisition of the material for permanent display at Harborough Museum, the project provides an excellent model for the future investigation of other open-air ritual sites. This will surely be one of its most enduring legacies.

It has been a real privilege for all of us at the School of Archaeology & Ancient History – and especially myself, as an archaeologist with a particular interest in Iron Age Britain – to have been involved in this exemplary and internationally significant archaeological project in our own region.

Professor Colin Haselgrove
University of Leicester

Introduction

Treasure is usually associated with precious metal items of high intrinsic value. The huge number of gold and silver coins, the Roman helmet and other metal objects found at Hallaton in Leicestershire caught the public's imagination as a treasure find when it was announced to the press in 2003.

However, the story of the Hallaton Treasure goes way beyond that of a simple metal-detector find, with surprises at every turn. Although the artefacts are spectacular and can themselves provide vast amounts of information, it was the subsequent thorough investigation of the findspot and surrounding landscape that has enabled archaeologists to piece together the story of why these finds were buried on a hilltop in rural south-east Leicestershire.

Iron Age coin hoards, a silver helmet and other artefacts, as well as masses of pig bones combine to tell the story of rituals that happened here 2000 years ago. Thanks to this discovery, we have had completely to rethink our ideas about this region and its inhabitants in the period before and just after the coming of the Romans.

The preservation and investigation of the area around the first finds was largely due to the hard work of Ken Wallace and the Hallaton Field Work Group, who not only made the initial discovery but also understood the importance of reporting the find to the right people and keeping the discovery a secret. The group has been involved in every aspect of the project from digging on site, to sieving the soil for the thousands of animal bones recovered.

After a decade of conservation and study, the artefacts have now returned to Leicestershire. It was always the intention to try and display the finds close to where they were found and with help from the British Museum and the Heritage Lottery Fund this was achieved with a newly refurbished display in Harborough Museum, a display in the Hallaton Museum and a travelling exhibition, with those involved giving talks at events and training sessions all over Britain.

Some of the museum displays featuring the treasure. Hallaton Museum (above) tells the story of the discovery and subsequent dig, while most of the finds are on display at Harborough Museum (the original Harborough displays are shown below). Photographs courtesy of Harborough and Hallaton Museums.

The Discovery

It was a cold winter's day in 2000 when the Hallaton Field Work Group (HFWG) first set foot on the fields overlooking the village of Hallaton in Leicestershire. They were walking over ploughed fields, as they did most weekends, looking for fragments of pottery and flint that could tell them about the history of their local area.

At first that there was nothing about this particular field to suggest it was any different to the many others the group had already walked. Their fieldwalking showed that Iron Age people had lived in the area over 2000 years ago, followed by the Romans who had built roads, farmsteads and villas. The scatters of late Iron Age and Roman pottery that they were picking up in this field suggested that this could be another settlement site. They found animal bones too, although these were thought to be the remains of animals buried by the farmer, as ancient bones do not usually survive well in ploughed fields.

However, it was these bones that led one member of the group, Ken Wallace, to seek permission to return to the field with his metal detector. Going back to the point at the top of the small hill where the bones had been picked up, Ken started to detect and was shocked to find several tiny silver coins in the ploughed surface. At the end of that first day detecting, Ken took his finds home to show to his wife Hazel. 'I asked him if they were Celtic,' she recalls. 'When he said they were I couldn't believe it. There were so many. I knew that you never normally find more than one or two.'

Ken's delight at finding the first coins quickly turned into panic. After several days there were more than 200 silver coins piled up on their kitchen table and many more still out on the field.

When Ken Wallace turned up on a field near Hallaton with his metal detector, he had no idea that he was about to start on a journey that would end up with one of the most important archaeological discoveries in Britain. Ken and his wife Hazel were members of the Hallaton Field Work Group, one of many Leicestershire-based groups who spend their weekends searching ploughed fields for evidence of the past.

As well as having being a keen fieldwalker for more than 20 years, Ken was also an amateur metal detectorist, systematically detecting many of the fields walked by the group, although so far he hadn't found anything more exciting than two Bronze Age axe-heads and a handful of Roman artefacts and coins.

The reason that we now have so much information about the site is because Ken and Hazel recognized the importance of what they had found. Rather than carry on collecting the coins themselves, they got experts involved, allowing archaeological excavations to reveal the story behind the burial of the coins.

Ken and Hazel, realising that their find was highly unusual and that there could be even more important finds buried under the ground, took the coins to show Peter Liddle, Leicestershire's Community Archaeologist. Peter remembers his amazement as Ken slowly trickled a few of the tiny silver coins into his hand. He was even more astonished when Ken produced a bag containing dozens more coins and calmly informed him that there were plenty more still out on the field (*left*) waiting to be picked up!

Knowing that the coins were subject to the 1996 Treasure Act, Ken, aided by Peter, informed the Coroner about the finds, which were then sent to experts at the British Museum, where they were identified as late Iron Age coins produced between about 50 BC and AD 50. They were types made by the Corieltavi, the Iron Age inhabitants of the East Midlands. Due to the sheer quantity and condition of the finds, Jonathan Williams at the British Museum suggested that they might have come from a shrine, where offerings such as coins were made. This practice began in the Iron Age, before the Roman conquest, and continued into the Roman period.

It was obvious that help was needed to investigate the findspot and determine how best to protect it. English Heritage was approached and, recognising that such a rich site was vulnerable to illegal metal detecting, agreed to fund some work. The local archaeological unit – University of Leicester Archaeological Services (ULAS) was asked to undertake the fieldwork. A strategy involving more fieldwalking and metal detecting, geophysical survey and excavation was produced, in order to discover more about the coins and the reasons behind their burial.

Ken was worried that if news of the coins became public, the site would be threatened by illicit metal detecting. The Coroner's office agreed that the Inquest to determine the status of the finds would only take place after the planned fieldwork, in order to keep the location a secret. The weather made further work on the field impossible, but to stop for the winter meant leaving a highly visible site close to the road vulnerable to destructive raids by thieves. Work was further impeded the following year by bad weather. However, potential thieves were not the only problem. In early 2001, the outbreak of Foot and Mouth Disease restricted access to the countryside. All archaeological work was delayed and Ken could only watch as the crops grew taller and hope that nobody would plunder the site over the summer. Serious work could not be resumed until the autumn. Amazingly, in spite of all this, the secret was kept – not even the fieldwalkers' own children knew about the site! This was just as well, for the field, which had already yielded hundreds of Iron Age coins, was soon to reveal that it contained thousands more. From the very start, the HFWG were involved in the dig. When finally the restrictions were lifted, almost a year after the first coins were found, Site Director Vicki Score and a small team of archaeologists met with Ken and the other members of the HFWG in autumn 2001, and fieldwork could begin.

Hazel Wallace

'When Ken brought the first coins back I was amazed at how tiny and how beautiful they were. We spread them out on the kitchen table to look at the dish-shaped coins with their disjointed horses and imagined the Iron Age people who made them all those years ago.'

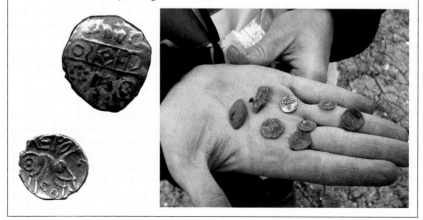

Left: The ploughed field in Hallaton where it all began.
Right: Some of the Iron Age coins as they came out of the ground. Above: Coins cleaned for display. Photographs courtesy of Chris Royall.

Treasure – Who Owns the Past?

Before 1996 the ownership of valuable objects was determined by an ancient law dating back to the 12th century. An object was considered to be 'Treasure Trove' and therefore the property of the Crown, if it was made of more than 50% gold or silver and if the original owners or heirs were unknown. Treasure also had to have been hidden with the intention to recover it later. If there had been no such intention (for example if it was placed in a grave) or if the object had simply been lost or abandoned, the treasure would belong either to the first person who found it or the landowner.

The problems with this law became apparent following the excavation of the Anglo-Saxon burial mounds at Sutton Hoo in 1939. Because the treasure formed part of a magnificent boat burial, the objects were not 'Treasure Trove' and therefore belonged to the landowner, Mrs Edith May Pretty. Fortunately, she was keen that everyone should share in the excitement of the discovery and generously donated the finds to the nation. Other objects were declared not to be treasure because they didn't contain a high enough proportion of silver or gold.

Many items not considered 'Treasure Trove' were sold for exorbitant prices and sometimes left the country. It was realised that a change was needed and the old law was replaced by the Treasure Act in 1996. This did away with the idea that there had to be an intention to recover the objects and also ensured that material found in association with treasure also qualified – for example the animal bones found alongside the coins at Hallaton. This change and the introduction of a national recording scheme has had a remarkable effect on the nation's heritage not only in the numbers of finds being recorded but also in allowing museums to acquire important archaeological material.

Metal detecting and archaeologists

In the 1970s lightweight metal detectors (which had been developed from machines used by the military to detect land-mines) became widely available and the new hobby of metal detecting quickly attracted those hoping to find their own 'treasure'. Unfortunately a few people took this hobby further by raiding known archaeological sites at night. Known as Nighthawks, they not only removed objects but also often damaged buried remains. The destruction of several important archaeological sites gave rise to a mutual distrust between detectorists and archaeologists.

Alarmed by the rise in popularity of this hobby, archaeologists saw many metal detectorists as treasure hunters seeking to destroy and sell on the nation's heritage. Campaigns such as STOP (Stop Taking Our Past) tried to persuade the public against metal detecting. Unfortunately this simply increased the antagonism between the two groups, with the many 'legal' detectorists regarding archaeologists as obstructive and wanting to keep all knowledge of their excavations and finds to themselves. Fortunately both sides came to realise that they could benefit from sharing techniques and information. The 1996 Treasure Act and the accompanying Portable Antiquities Scheme have encouraged archaeologists and metal detectorists to work together.

Leicestershire has a strong tradition of local community archaeology, and professional archaeologists frequently ask local metal detectorists to assist them during excavations. This was very much the case at Hallaton, where the HFWG provided all of the metal detecting during the excavations and even helped to train ULAS staff on how best to use the machines to find different types of objects.

The Portable Antiquities Scheme

The Portable Antiquities Scheme – or PAS – is a hugely successful scheme set up to identify and record archaeological objects found by members of the public all over England and Wales.

The PAS has enabled finders to learn more about the objects they have discovered and what light they can shed on the past. It has been a major success in encouraging people to report their discoveries. Although treasure objects capture the most attention, lots of other finds can also tell us about the past. Every year thousands of objects are discovered by walkers and detectorists and added to the PAS database, providing an important source of information for archaeologists and interested members of the public alike.

What should I do if I find Treasure?

All finds of Treasure must be reported to the Coroner for the district in which they are found within 14 days of the day on which you made the discovery, or within 14 days after the day on which you realised the find might be treasure. Advice can be obtained from your local Finds Liaison Officer (*see page 64*).

Keeping the Secret

The discovery of the Hallaton treasure was one of the best-kept secrets of its time. Normally with valuable finds such as this word leaks out within a matter of weeks. Other large coin hoards such as those from Wanborough, Surrey (possibly more than 10,000 coins) or the Bowl hoard from Norfolk (more than 8,000 coins) were dug up and taken away without being reported within a short space of time. Everyone concerned realised the success of the Hallaton project was dependent on keeping the location of the site as quiet as possible. HFWG members and ULAS staff even attended the Celtic Coin Conference in Oxford and sat quietly pretending just to be interested amateurs. Listening to the speakers, it dawned on them how few coins from the East Midlands were known. With thousands of coins still preserved in their original burial place, it was clear that the discovery at Hallaton was going to turn everything on its head and the group were determined to protect the site until all the coins could be removed from the ground safely.

Their efforts paid off and the initial excavations were carried out without disturbance. The fact that the coins and other finds were legally recovered under controlled archaeological conditions is one of the most important aspects of the work. However, in April 2003 after two seasons of excavations, the inquest was held and it was impossible to keep the find quiet any longer. It was announced to the media with a display at the British Museum, and with coverage in national and international newspapers and magazines. For the archaeologists and HFWG members alike, it was a relief to be able to discuss the finds publicly and several group members were featured on the local radio and TV news and (Ken even appeared on ITV's Richard and Judy).

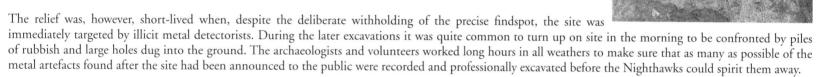

The relief was, however, short-lived when, despite the deliberate withholding of the precise findspot, the site was immediately targeted by illicit metal detectorists. During the later excavations it was quite common to turn up on site in the morning to be confronted by piles of rubbish and large holes dug into the ground. The archaeologists and volunteers worked long hours in all weathers to make sure that as many as possible of the metal artefacts found after the site had been announced to the public were recorded and professionally excavated before the Nighthawks could spirit them away.

The local community was also determined to try and prevent any more objects being stolen and set up a rota to check the field for intruders; everyone in the village was on the alert for unusual cars or visitors lurking nearby. Motion-detectors were installed that sent an alarm to mobile phones and night after night group members would rush up to the field with the local police to scare away groups of thieves trying to raid the site under the cover of darkness.

How many coins and artefacts were stolen from the site can never be known, but unlike Wanborough, at least the archaeologists had managed to excavate a good proportion of the site before any Nighthawks got to it. Today an agreement between Leicestershire County Council and the landowner means that the area has been put back to pasture. Without continued ploughing turning over the soil and bringing any remaining finds to the surface there is little reason for detectorists to return to the site. It also means that the remaining archaeology is safe from plough damage and preserved for future generations.

Above: Surveying the damage done by illegal metal detecting at Hallaton overnight.
Left: Ken was instrumental in teaching the ULAS archaeologists the art of metal detecting.

Geophysical Survey

Above: Using a fluxgate gradiometer.

Following the discovery the first stage of the investigation was to undertake a geophysical survey across the site and its surroundings. This would, it was hoped, pick up any archaeological features associated with the coins and perhaps show if there were any hoards still buried beneath the soil.

The most obvious features on the survey are the dark lines formed by enclosure ditches (red on the interpretation opposite). There seems to be one large enclosure to the south with several smaller enclosures within it. The northern side of the large enclosure forms the southern boundary of another enclosure. Several of these ditches have since been excavated and found to contain Roman pottery from the 1st to 4th centuries AD. Within the enclosures are numerous dark 'blobs' (shaded blue on the interpretation). These are pits containing pottery, brick, tile, animal bone and other rubbish, and also date to the Roman period. The green circular features (approximately 10–12m across) are probably roundhouses. The survey confirmed what the fieldwalking pottery had suggested – a late Iron Age/early Roman settlement in the 1st century AD (indicated by the roundhouses) followed by Roman occupation dating from the late 1st—2nd century and continuing into the 4th century AD. Perhaps surprisingly, the area where the coins were found (marked by the red star) was blank and all of the features showing on the survey that were excavated seem to be later in date than the early 1st century AD coins.

The magenta circle south-east of the site is slightly larger (16m) and although this has not been excavated it may well be a Bronze Age round barrow. Bronze Age metalwork has been found nearby.

How does geophysical survey work?
Geophysical survey is a non-destructive method used by archaeologists to look for features beneath the soil. It is a quick and cost-effective way to map archaeological features and help target where best to dig. A large area around the coin hoards was surveyed using magnetometry. This measures variations in the earth's magnetic field that indicate the presence of archaeological remains in the ground.

Buried objects: Objects that have been heated to high temperatures (e.g. ceramic and iron objects) have their magnetic properties changed. These are called 'thermoremanent' effects, which are easily detected by magnetometers – buried features such as brick walls, foundations, steel or clay pipes, hearths, kilns and ferrous metal will all stand out from the 'background' levels.

'Cut' features: Topsoil is generally more magnetic than subsoil or the underlying natural, because it contains decomposed or burnt particles. Ditches and pits that have been dug in the past and subsequently filled up with soil will show up on a survey as a highly magnetic anomaly, i.e. a darker line on the plot. Similarly, where an old embankment has been ploughed out leaving a zone of thinner topsoil, a linear low magnetism feature can be detected, showing as a lighter line. These effects are clearly visible in the image to the right, where darker and lighter parallel lines indicate the ploughed out ridges and furrows left by medieval cultivation on the hill.

Above: One of the Roman ditches identified from the geophysical survey. The dark soil of the ditch shows up as a dark line on the geophysical survey (left).

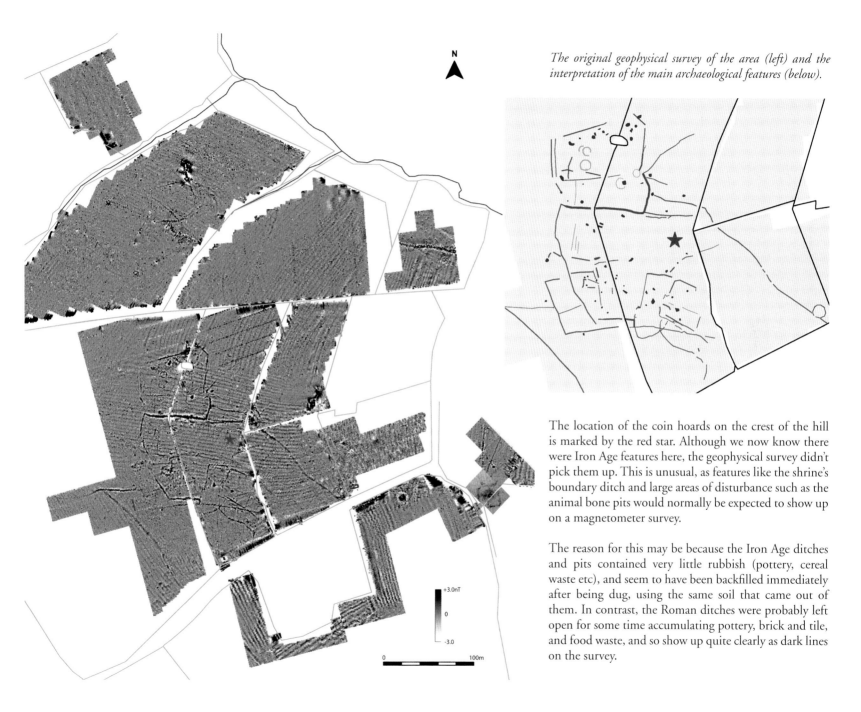

The original geophysical survey of the area (left) and the interpretation of the main archaeological features (below).

+3.0nT

0

-3.0

0   100m

The location of the coin hoards on the crest of the hill is marked by the red star. Although we now know there were Iron Age features here, the geophysical survey didn't pick them up. This is unusual, as features like the shrine's boundary ditch and large areas of disturbance such as the animal bone pits would normally be expected to show up on a magnetometer survey.

The reason for this may be because the Iron Age ditches and pits contained very little rubbish (pottery, cereal waste etc), and seem to have been backfilled immediately after being dug, using the same soil that came out of them. In contrast, the Roman ditches were probably left open for some time accumulating pottery, brick and tile, and food waste, and so show up quite clearly as dark lines on the survey.

Finding the First Hoards

Nine trial trenches were dug to target some of the strong anomalies shown on the geophysical survey. All of these turned out to be Roman features of much later date than the Iron Age coins. Curiously, the survey had failed to find anything that looked like 'archaeology' in the area that the coins were coming from. It was thought that the coins Ken had found came from the top of a buried hoard or hoards that had been caught and dragged into the soil by ploughing. It seemed unlikely that excavation was going to find much beyond a few more coins and – if we were very lucky – the base of the hoard still *in situ*.

The tenth trench was therefore located where Ken said most of the coins had been found. Ken had been meticulous about the precise recording of his metal-detected finds and had gridded up the field and plotted every coin to the nearest metre. Armed with this 'treasure map', site director Vicki Score was able to pinpoint a good location for the trench.

No sooner had the JCB started to remove the topsoil than a lump of something green was spotted in the trench. A quick inspection confirmed it was a group of coins (the copper content of the silver coins had leached out, staining them green). Not wanting to draw attention to the hoard, it was immediately covered with a plastic bag and digging continued. More coin hoards were quickly found and dealt with in the same manner. Questions from the JCB driver were answered by saying they were just bits of iron in the soil. Finally at lunchtime the archaeologists and Ken were able to send the JCB to another part of the field and take a closer look at what had been unearthed.

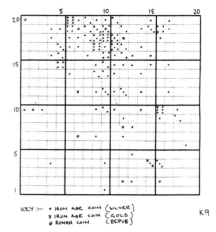

Above: Ken's Treasure Map.

There were six green blobs covered with finds bags in the small trench and Ken was convinced that there were strong signals from his detector indicating more hoards still waiting to be found. It was rapidly realised that these discoveries were even more important than had been anticipated and the archaeologists and Ken agreed that the finds had to be kept between themselves to prevent any word getting out that might lead to the site being targeted by Nighthawks. Decisions then had to be made as to what to do with the hoards already uncovered. The presence of a JCB on the hilltop close to a public footpath had already drawn some attention from walkers and it was feared that the coins might be gone the next morning if they were left overnight, so the archaeologists decided that as many of the hoards as possible should be lifted that afternoon.

Vicki Score, ULAS Site Director

'I honestly hadn't expected to find anything in the trench. It was quite a shock when I spotted the first flash of green and realised what it was. It was an even greater shock when several more turned up. All I could do was throw finds bags over them and pretend they weren't anything important. By the time the sixth hoard was uncovered I was starting to panic about how we were going to deal with them and I stopped the machine and sent the driver across the field to tidy some spoil heaps.'

Ken Wallace

'I'd been metal detecting along the top of the field. As I walked towards the hedge for dinner Vicki called me over to the trench. She pointed to several finds bags lying on the surface and told me to go and look under one. I lifted the bag and saw a small pile of coins. Although I'd picked up hundreds of stray coins by then it gave me a real sense of wonder to see the hoards preserved in the soil where they had been buried all those years ago.'

Opening the trench. To prevent news about the find from spreading the archaeologists even kept the discovery secret from the JCB driver.

Above: The coin hoards in the ground. Although these hoards comprise mostly silver coins they contain some copper, which has corroded, and this is why they appear green.

Having made the decision to get the coins out of the ground as soon as possible, the next step was to determine exactly how best to do this. It was vitally important to record as much as possible about each hoard before it was removed from the ground.

The site was obviously damaged. The hundreds of coins found by Ken in the ploughsoil had been dislodged from the tops of the hoards, but the bases of these hoards were still very much *in situ*, untouched since the day they had been placed in the ground. It was essential that they were removed as carefully as possible to preserve their archaeological integrity.

Fortunately the soil that the hoards were buried in was very clayey. By digging carefully around each coin group, it would be possible to lift each one in a block of soil. In this way the hoards could be removed rapidly while keeping their structure intact so that they could be excavated properly once safely back in the laboratory.

Before the coins were lifted each group was cleaned and photographed and its position marked on a plan. Any loose coins were removed from the top of the hoard and their locations carefully marked on the bags. Finally with all the recording finished the delicate task of digging up the hoards began.

Above: One of the coin blocks still in its clay soil matrix after it was lifted out of the ground.

The archaeologists carefully excavated around each of the hoards, leaving a block of soil containing coins. Once they were happy that they had gone deep enough, a spade was carefully slid underneath, and the solid block of soil containing the coins was removed and placed in boxes ready to be transported to the laboratories.

Back at the University, the archaeologists showed their boxes and bags of coins to stunned colleagues. No one had ever seen so many Iron Age coins in one place before and everyone wanted to see the finds. How would it be best to handle the site? The need for secrecy was impressed on everyone concerned. It was decided that work on site should continue as normal, but Leicester County Council, the British Museum and English Heritage would be informed and a strategy for dealing with the site would be prepared.

The Excavations

It was obvious that the small trench containing the coin hoards needed to be extended. Not only was Ken adamant more coins were to be found, but a ditch had also been identified at the edge of the trench, suggesting that the hoards might after all be associated with other features. It now seemed very likely indeed that the coins had been deposited at a late Iron Age shrine or ritual site and represented offerings to the gods. In view of the vulnerability of the site to both theft and further ploughing, English Heritage immediately agreed that the excavation area should be enlarged. Experts from the British Museum confirmed that lifting the coins in blocks was the best method, with any loose coins being bagged and kept with the relevant block. A revised project design was drawn up and more archaeologists and the rest of the HFWG were brought in to help with digging.

The excavations were carried out over three seasons. After consulting Ken's coin plots overlain on the geophysical survey, it was decided that for the best possible chance of finding any archaeological features or layers associated with the hoards, the trench should be increased to 25m x 30m. This area was opened in 2001 funded by English Heritage. In 2003 further areas to the north, south, east and west of the first trench were examined, funded by the BBC (who were making a television programme about treasure), the British Museum and ULAS. In 2005 ULAS and the HFWG undertook some small hand-dug trenches targeted at specific features within the site. Work was also carried out in 2008–9 by the University of Leicester and the HFWG investigating the late Iron Age and Roman settlement to the north of the shrine.

All of the finds (with the exception of those found on the spoil heaps) were recorded in 3D. The sheer quantity of finds and the intricacy and fragility of many of the deposits made for time-consuming and labour-intensive work. Fortunately the HFWG were more than willing to work alongside the archaeologists not just on site (often in appalling weather), but also washing finds and sieving the many bags of clay that were collected from the site (*below*).

Once the extended trench had been cleaned over, it became obvious that the six coin hoards from the original small trench were not an isolated find. As well as several more hoards, a ditch was identified running north–south with an entrance to the east, along with several other features. None of these had appeared on the geophysical survey.

The first priority was to remove the remaining coin hoards. By now a total of fourteen individual hoards had been identified, clustered in one small area next to the entrance. These were each cleaned, photographed and recorded. When the coin hoards had been removed from site, work began on cleaning the rest of the trench and investigating the archaeological features.

The north–south ditch was identified as a boundary ditch marking the eastern side of the shrine. The coins had been buried just inside the entrance. In the middle of the entranceway, the body of a dog had been buried in the top of a shallow pit. Part of the skeleton had been destroyed by a land drain but it was clear that the dog had been carefully 'posed', as if looking towards the coin hoards placed at the entrance to the shrine to protect the treasure inside.

Above: The metal detector remained a key tool throughout the excavations, with Ken and his fellow detectorists working closely with the archaeologists.

Digging with metal detectors

The ULAS archaeologists soon realised that they would have to adapt many of their usual practices for this site. The Hallaton detectorists were a vital part of the investigation and they were having problems with all the metal that is normally used on an excavation. Grid pegs, section nails and nails for holding down context and finds tags all had to be exchanged for plastic pegs to avoid false readings. The archaeologists soon learnt that standing next to someone detecting while wearing steel toe-capped boots was definitely out, and everybody quickly understood that rings and watches were not ideal when helping out with the metal detecting.

Above: Digging the dog skeleton in the entranceway, looking south along the boundary ditch.

At the same time Ken and his fellow detectorists also had to adapt their practices to working on an archaeological dig. The first lesson was learning not to tread on a freshly trowelled area, no matter how good a reading there was! And of course working over a newly cleaned archaeological site meant that they couldn't just dig up their finds as soon as they found them. A system was developed using different types of tags for iron, silver and other metals with extra tags used for larger objects. When features were ready to be excavated, detectorists and archaeologists worked as a team to make sure that the objects were recovered without destroying the context, and that the context was dug without missing any objects.

Leicestershire on the Eve of the Roman Invasion

Extensive fieldwalking, excavation and survey over the last few decades has drastically improved our knowledge of Iron Age Leicestershire prior to the coming of the Romans in AD 43. Archaeologists had previously thought that the East Leicestershire claylands were heavily wooded and not particularly suitable for cultivation, suggesting that the area probably wasn't settled until the Middle Ages. However, now we know otherwise. The fieldwalking and geophysical surveys undertaken by the HFWG and other local community groups, as well as excavations by commercial archaeology units have uncovered a wealth of evidence hidden beneath the rolling hills and ploughed fields of Leicestershire. It is now clear that this region was occupied from prehistoric times onwards. Aerial photography and geophysical survey have identified a landscape full of farmsteads (both enclosed and unenclosed), with their associated fields and trackways, suggesting that the whole area was extensively occupied in the last centuries BC.

Most people seem to have lived in roundhouses. These were large enough for a family to live in and those identified by geophysical survey and excavation at Hallaton, to the north of the shrine, were 10–12m in diameter. Walls were constructed using timber posts infilled with wattle and daub panels, and the buildings had a conical thatched roof. Many Leicestershire roundhouses had eavesdrip gullies around the outside to catch and drain away rainwater dripping off the roof. The economy seems to have been mainly pastoral-based with sheep/goat, cattle and pigs being the most common animals found on domestic sites. Droveways and enclosures suggest that stock control was being practised and sheep would have been kept for their wool as well as for meat, and cattle used to pull ploughs and carts. Cereals such as spelt, barley and wheat found on excavated sites and the presence of querns indicate that the Iron Age people also cultivated cereals, threshed them and ground them into flour.

Increasingly in the late Iron Age houses were enclosed by ditches and linked to neighbouring fields by trackways. Settlements varied in size; while most of the scattered settlements in the Hallaton area would have been fairly small, single family dwellings, excavations in Leicester and Humberstone have revealed much larger communities of perhaps several hundred people. Unlike the vast defensive complexes known in the south of England, there are relatively few hillforts in the East Midlands. Burrough Hill is one example and excavations there by the University of Leicester suggest that the fort could have been a centre for commerce and trade as well as a large settlement. By the end of the late Iron Age small 'proto-towns' start to emerge at places such as Leicester, Great Casterton, Thistleton and Medbourne, supporting slightly larger populations and serving as local points of contact and trade.

Above: How the late Iron Age settlement at Hallaton might have looked. © Leicestershire County Council.

Reconstructed roundhouse at Groby, Leicestershire.

The Romans in Leicestershire

The Romans advancing northwards after the invasion in AD 43 would have encountered an agricultural landscape with frequent farmsteads and some larger settlements resembling villages. *Ratae* (the Roman name for Leicester derives from the Celtic word for 'ramparts') had only developed into a town at the end of the Iron Age, but high quality pottery and imported artefacts indicate contact and trade links with the Roman world. Roman objects would have already been circulating in Iron Age Leicestershire for some time before the arrival of the legions.

It is possible that a Roman military fort was built at Leicester in the early years of the conquest. At the same time the native settlement there appears to have continued to thrive and under Roman rule was soon recognised as the *civitas* capital (administrative centre) of the local tribe, the Corieltavi.

Many Roman rural sites appear to have Iron Age origins and some settlements continued into the 2nd century and beyond, suggesting that Roman culture was quickly assimilated into the domestic lifestyle of the inhabitants.

© Leicestershire County Council.

The Corieltavi

Roman sources tell us that there were around seventeen major tribes living in England and Wales. The main group of people living in the East Midlands were identified by the Romans as the Corieltavi, a name meaning 'army of the many rivers'. Roman coins and objects found among the Hallaton finds demonstrate that the Corieltavi had at least some contact with the Roman world. In the south of England, Iron Age chieftains were rising in power and influence at the end of the Iron Age, and were in contact with and even sometimes supported by the Romans.

Study of the Hallaton coins suggests that the Corieltavi were not a single cohesive tribe with one ruler, but were more likely to be a mix of smaller groups with local leaders and chieftains held together via networks of allegiances and family loyalties. These smaller units were probably self-sufficient groups sharing some resources such as pasture and woodlands. The Hallaton shrine may have been a meeting place where these groups could gather to maintain social contacts and to worship their gods.

Whether the Corieltavi were pro- or anti-Roman is not clear. Defences built at *Ratae* (Leicester) just before the conquest might suggest that some local people were expecting to resist the Romans. The burial of precious coins and objects at the Hallaton shrine at around the time of the conquest might indicate a period of uncertainty and fear and a need for protection from the gods. However, the presence of Roman objects at Hallaton and the gradual emergence of early Roman settlements out of later Iron Age sites might suggest that many natives were tolerant of the invaders and possibly even regarded them as allies.

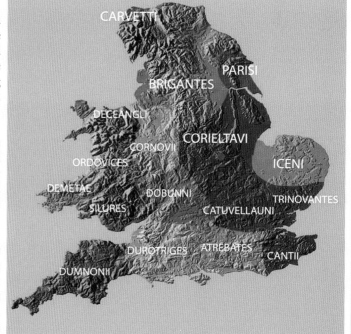

Above: The Iron Age tribes of Britain with the shrine marked as a red dot. © Leicestershire County Council.

The History of Hallaton

Hallaton is a picturesque village lying just over 20km south-east of Leicester. Although today it is relatively small, the church was probably the site of a minster before the Norman Conquest and in the 12th century Hallaton was defended by a motte and bailey castle. In the Middle Ages, Hallaton became a prosperous market town with four annual fairs, and by the 14th century was probably the economic centre for much of the south-eastern part of the county, continuing to hold fairs into the 18th century. It was only with the rise of Market Harborough that the village began to decline in importance.

The earliest evidence of human activity comes from finds of stone axes and scatters of flint indicating that prehistoric communities were active in the area. By the Iron Age the remains of enclosures and pottery scatters demonstrate widespread occupation around Hallaton, Medbourne, Slawston, Blaston and Stonton Wyville. By the time the Hallaton shrine was in use in the mid 1st century AD, the whole region was well settled. The site itself lies on a ridge overlooking the village to the north and the Welland valley to the south and was well placed to attract communities from across south-east Leicestershire.

This area was well served by Roman roads. The Gartree Road ran from Leicester into Northamptonshire through the Roman small town of Medbourne. The Roman towns at Market Harborough and Medbourne and several nearby villa sites have all produced finds suggesting that they originated in the late Iron Age. Other local evidence for activity at this date comes from a small hoard of Iron Age coins found in a probable Roman marching camp overlooking the river at Weston by Welland (Northamptonshire) – supporting the idea that the whole area was already occupied when the Romans arrived.

Although Roman pottery was mainly supplied to the Hallaton area from the Nene Valley, near modern Peterborough, 15 miles to the east, small-scale production has been identified more locally. Fragments of kiln bars (ceramic bars used to support the pots in the kiln) have been found near Hallaton. Kilns are often located close to suitable sources of raw materials, and the local woodland would have been managed as an important resource for raising of pigs, as well as providing wood for building and fuel.

Despite the wealth of archaeological evidence that Hallaton lay in a rich archaeological landscape, it is astonishing that there was no hint of the ritual site on a hilltop above the village just waiting to be discovered.

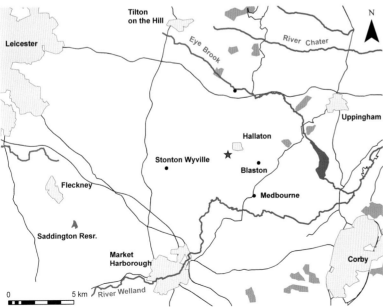

Above left: The butter cross in the centre of Hallaton village. Left: The location of the site (red star). Opposite: some of the Iron Age and Roman sites in the area.

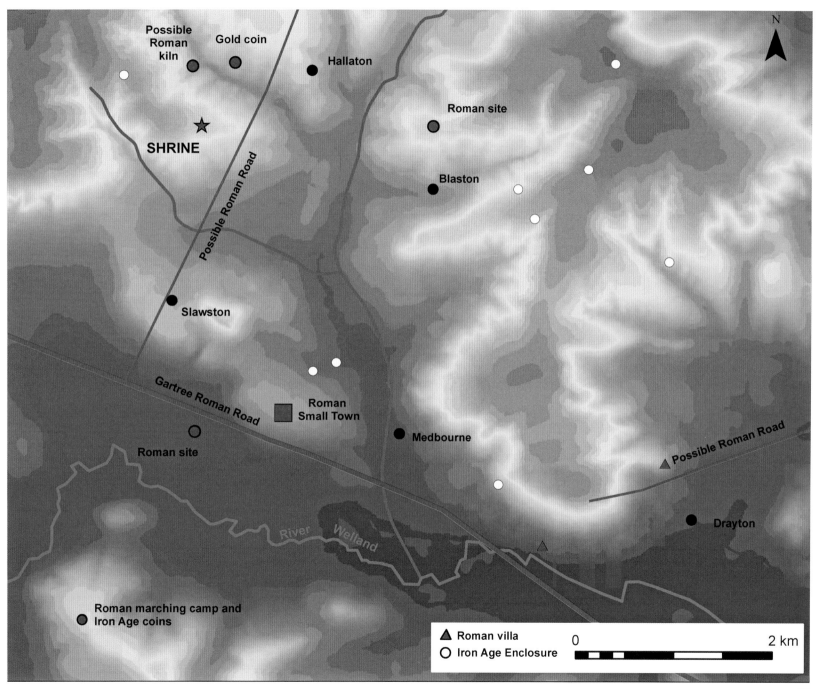

Possible Roman kiln

Gold coin

Hallaton

Roman site

SHRINE

Possible Roman Road

Blaston

Slawston

Gartree Roman Road

Roman Small Town

Possible Roman Road

Roman site

Medbourne

River Welland

Drayton

Roman marching camp and Iron Age coins

▲ Roman villa

○ Iron Age Enclosure

0 2 km

N

The Layout of the Site

After three seasons of excavations the plan of the site became clear. The shrine occupied the crest of the hill and was marked off by a ditch running north–south, with an entrance to the east. The ditch terminated a short distance to the north, but continued beyond the excavations to the south. The entrance appeared to have been carefully constructed with a slot in the centre forming a sort of 'turnstile'. The remnants of a trackway surfaced with small pebbles led up to and through the entrance. Fourteen coin hoards had been deposited near one another in the northern part of the entrance. The bodies of two dogs had been buried in the entrance slot at different times. A pit to the south contained another large coin hoard along with carefully buried parts of Roman helmets. Metalwork including a silver bowl and two ingots had been deliberately placed in the southern ditch, with the remains of a third dog found nearby, along with other animal bones.

Nothing was found within what seems to be the interior of the shrine except for a small undated pit; in fact this area was remarkably devoid of finds. Outside the shrine, however, was a different story. A badly disturbed circular slot may have been an early round building – perhaps the original focus of the shrine? Directly opposite the entrance was a mass of animal bones (later identified as pigs). Parts of dismembered animals had been placed in several pits and a spread of bones above may have been made up of discarded bones dumped as rubbish.

The site was also used in the Roman period. Ditches, pits, building debris and trackways were all uncovered in the southern part of the trench, overlying the boundary ditch. However, the main ritual area seems to have been carefully avoided, despite its ideal location on the crest of the hill. Perhaps the later inhabitants knew about the shrine and were wary of desecrating it and bringing down the wrath of the Iron Age gods.

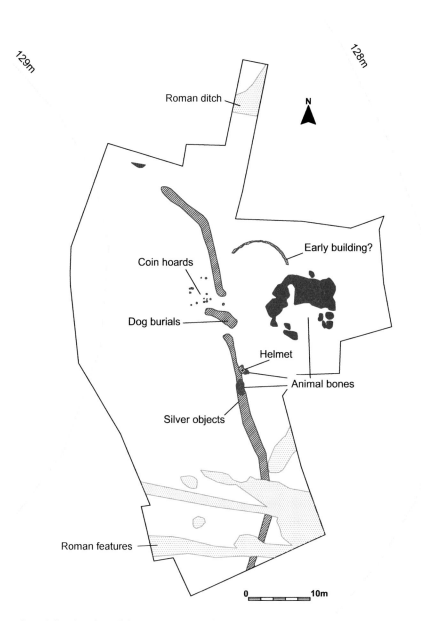

129m
128m

Roman ditch

N

Coin hoards

Early building?

Dog burials

Helmet

Animal bones

Silver objects

Roman features

0   10m

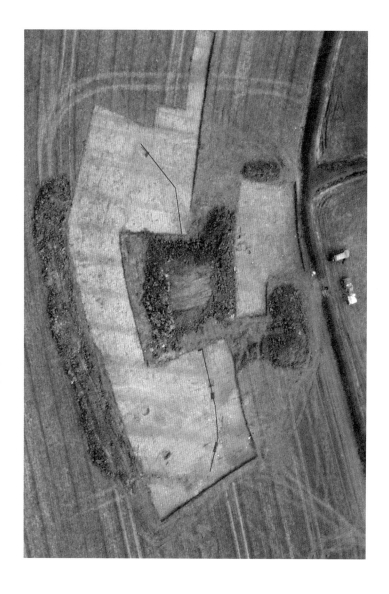

Above left: The plan of the main excavated area of the site.
Above right: Aerial view of the site in the second season of excavation. The entrance and coin hoards lie beneath the spoil heap in the centre. The red line shows the boundary ditch. Evidence for medieval ploughing can be seen in the parallel lines of ridge and furrow running roughly west to east across the trench. Photograph courtesy of Chris Royall.

Artist's reconstruction of the entranceway showing the location of the key deposits. © Leicestershire County Council.

Boundaries to Another World

Boundaries became an increasingly important part of late Iron Age societies, with the open landscapes of earlier prehistory giving way to a more visibly enclosed landscape. Ditches were used to surround houses and to define different areas of activity, and ditch systems and pit alignments were used to demarcate large communal spaces. Boundaries and entrances seem to have been particularly important and often contained objects, particularly coins.

Only an eastern boundary was uncovered on the hilltop at Hallaton. The plan of the ditch seems to have been polygonal with the entranceway approximately one third of the way down the eastern side. Polygonal boundaries are an unusual feature in the Iron Age, when enclosure ditches are more likely to be curving or rectangular in plan. However, the large enclosure at Snettisham (Norfolk), where dozens of Iron Age torcs were found, was polygonal in shape, and similar enclosures are found at some Roman temples.

The importance of the Hallaton ditch and its eastern entrance is shown by its relationship with the different groups of artefacts. Although it would have originally have been an open ditch, it was subsequently backfilled before the burial of the coins and helmet parts. Boundaries on ritual sites usually serve to define the transition from the sacred space inside to the normal outside world, as well as preventing access. The steepness of some sections of the ditch suggests that it could have held a wooden palisade or fence at some stage, screening the sacred space from view and making an impressive barrier. However boundaries did not always have to be substantial physical features – the simple knowledge that a boundary was associated with the gods might have been enough to keep people away. The northern part of the Hallaton ditch terminated after a short distance and probably would not have provided much of an obstacle to entry. Rather it might have represented both a spiritual link and a barrier to the world of the gods. It is of course possible that the boundary once continued around the entire hill top – perhaps in another form, such as a hedge. In the Iron Age, boundaries are often most impressive near an entrance.

The Hallaton ditch did not just mark out the area of sacred space but also itself became a focus for ritual activity. The coin hoards were deposited in a group to one side of the entrance, and the silver bowl, mount and ingots were all carefully arranged together with more coins in the ditch when it was backfilled. Animal bones were also deposited there and the placing of the helmet parts and yet more coins in a pit on the eastern edge of the ditch is surely no coincidence. The dogs buried at the entrance and in the ditch would have provided protection for their valuable contents.

Ditches are often considered to be *liminal* – a threshold between two opposing spheres of influence, each of which is significant in its own right. The ditch is an in-between place where neither force has precedence. The Hallaton ditch may mark the realm between the normal world and that of the gods; anything buried in it might be considered to provide a link between the two spheres.

Above: The Hallaton boundary ditch to the south of the entrance.

Guardian Dogs

The remains of three dogs were found at Hallaton. They had been treated very differently from the other animal bones and appear to be individual burials. The most complete skeleton was found in the top of the entrance slot. A second, earlier burial was also found in the same slot and the remains of a third dog were recovered from the boundary ditch.

The earlier dog in the entranceway was represented by only a few skull and neck bones. Its skeleton had been disturbed when the entrance slot was re-dug and the second dog buried there. More of the second dog skeleton survived, although its hind legs and back end had been truncated by the digging of a land drain. This dog had been deliberately placed in the top of the slot, and the way its legs were drawn back underneath it suggests that it had been bound. The dog's head was bent back so that it was pointing towards the hoards of coins – was this so that it could keep its eye on the treasure? Bones of a third dog found in the ditch close to the silver bowl and other objects perhaps watched over this section of the ditch and its contents.

In Roman times, dogs were fairly common in Britain and seem to have been kept as pets; there is evidence of breeding for smaller sizes. While the most obvious evidence for the presence of dogs comes from their skeletons on archaeological sites, there are also numerous examples of paw-prints left by dogs walking across drying tiles waiting to be fired.

Dogs in the Iron Age, however, would have probably have been kept chiefly as working animals used to herd stock, hunt and guard the farmstead, as well as for companionship. Hunting dogs were highly prized and the Greek historian Strabo tells us that the British exported dogs

> 'that are by nature suited to the purposes of the chase; the Celti, however, use both these and the native dogs for the purposes of war too.'

As well as being useful working animals, dogs play a unique role in their relationship with humans. That there has been a strong connection between dogs and humans for thousands of years is often illustrated on archaeological sites by their special treatment. While animals such as cows, sheep and pigs were used for their meat and skins, dogs seem to have been treated very differently, often appearing on ritual sites and accompanying human burials. Dogs were found on the Mesolithic site at Star Carr (dating to approximately 9000 BC). In the Bronze Age dogs were probably sacrificed at the wetland sites of Caldicot (Gwent) and Flag Fen (Cambridgeshire), and the special treatment of dogs continues into the Iron Age and Roman period.

Above: The dog in the entranceway had its legs pulled beneath the body as if bound and the held tilted so that it could watch over the coin hoards.

Below: Dog paw-prints on a Roman roof tile from Leicestershire. © Leicestershire County Council.

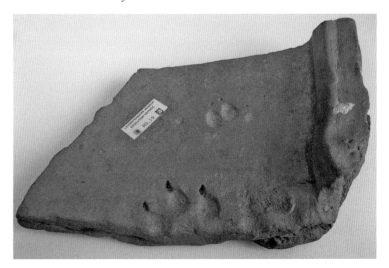

Above: Artist's impression of the Hallaton dog. © Leicestershire County Council.

In Iron Age Britain dogs were used for herding, hunting and war, and were probably selectively bred for these abilities. All three of the Hallaton dogs seem to be of a similar size – approximately 62cm from shoulder to ground. This is similar in height to a retriever or German Shepherd, and is relatively large compared to most other known Iron Age dogs.

The burial of dogs in pits and wells was common. Several dogs were deposited in a deep well near the shrine at Muntham Court (Sussex) and on a small Romano-British site at Staines (Middlesex) sixteen dogs were found in a well. At Danebury hillfort the bodies of two dogs were found in one of a series of pits belonging to the early phases outside the later defences. The bones of other animals had been interred with them, chalk blocks were then placed over the bodies and a timber structure erected over the top, all suggesting some kind of elaborate ritual.

There seems to be an association between dogs and doorways, perhaps symbolising the transition from one world to the next. Dogs have been found in the entrances to several hillforts including Maiden Castle (Dorset), where a dog buried in the centre of one of the entrances was interpreted as a guard dog. The Celtic hound god, Cunomaglus, was depicted as a dog guarding the underworld. This god was associated with hunting and healing; the saliva of dogs has long been known to have healing properties.

Dogs were also buried in Roman graves, presumably to accompany humans into the afterlife. At York Road, Leicester, a small dog, similar in size to a modern dachshund and probably a treasured pet, was interred in a full-size grave. At the Roman site at Silchester (Hampshire), there are half a dozen dog burials. One dog was interred with an infant and another was buried upright with the earth packed carefully around it; a knife from the same site had a handle in the form of two mating dogs. At another Roman cemetery at Lankhills, Winchester, one grave contained an empty coffin with a large dog apparently buried on the lid. All this suggests that dogs were used as guardians, a role that they were obviously suited for equally well in death as in life.

Nothing visible on the bones of the Hallaton dogs reveals how they were killed, although the bound legs of one animal might indicate that they were alive at the start of the ritual. Interestingly they all seem to be elderly animals with worn teeth and signs of age-related diseases. A favoured dog, near the end of its natural life, that had served the tribe well, may have been chosen to continue its service in the afterlife. Guardianship of the treasure at Hallaton may have been seen as a great honour awarded to faithful companions at the end of their lives.

The sacrifice and burial of the dogs suggests that the Iron Age people felt the site needed guarding. The dogs buried in the pit at the entrance perhaps protected the coins hoards that lay inside and prevented access to anyone likely to steal or harm the treasure – and perhaps also to welcome to those who were allowed into the shrine. The presence of two animals buried at different times suggests that when the entrance was modified, the protection had to be renewed. Perhaps something bad had happened and the shrine-builders felt that the dog's powers needed to be reinforced. Or possibly the protection offered by the first dog had expired and a new phase of activity at the shrine required a new sacrifice and burial. Similarly, the dog in the ditch could have been placed there to guard the silver objects buried there, as well as the helmet parts, which lay close by.

Their association with the ditch and the entrance might also suggest that dogs were suitable animals to 'inhabit' the boundary between the god's realm inside the shrine and that of everyday life outside. Perhaps their association with death and the underworld meant they could carry messages and convey the meaning of the rituals being enacted back to the gods that were being worshipped.

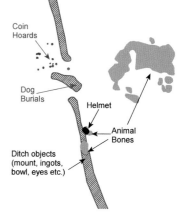

Coin Hoards

Dog Burials

Helmet

Animal Bones

Ditch objects (mount, ingots, bowl, eyes etc.)

The Hallaton Coins

Altogether, over five and a half thousand coins were found during the excavations. The vast majority of these were local types made by the Corieltavi in the decades before the Roman invasion, although some coins from other tribes (including the Catuvellauni whose lands lay to the south), and Republican and early Imperial Roman *denarii* were also present. At the time of the discovery, just over 3,000 Corieltavian coins were recorded from the whole country – which gives some idea of just how important this find was to the coin experts. The temptation when studying coins or other finds is to assume that what you have is representative of the rest. The Hallaton hoards have turned up several new types, as well as making coins once considered rare and exciting seem rather ordinary.

The coins came from three main areas on the site. A large hoard was buried in the pit with the helmet, with some coins interleaved between the helmet cheekpieces. Coins were also scattered in the ditch with the metalwork. Most of the coins however, came from fourteen individual hoards buried just inside the entrance. Despite careful cleaning, the archaeologists could see no obvious pits dug to contain these hoards. Either the pits were very small and immediately backfilled, with the clay pushed straight back into the hole after the coins had been placed there, or alternatively they were displayed in small open 'scoops' dug into the soil.

The Greek historian Diodorus Siculus, writing in the 1st century BC, describes the Gauls (the Iron Age inhabitants of France) offering gold, openly placed on the ground as a dedication to their gods. Julius Caesar also writes of the spoils of war being heaped in piles in temples and shrines. It seems that objects could be displayed openly in sacred places and fear of reprisal from the gods was enough to stop the treasure being looted.

A notable feature of the *in situ* entrance hoards was their shape. Iron Age coins tend to be slightly dished as a result of how they are made (*see page 31*). This means that they fit together easily in small groups. Many of the soil blocks show coins clustered together in a circle, suggesting that they were originally placed inside bags probably made from organic material that has long since rotted away leaving no trace.

Context

One of the most important things about the finds from this site is that so many of them retained their original archaeological 'context'. Over 60% of the Hallaton coins as well as many of the artefacts were still in their original burial place, with the remaining finds recovered from the ploughsoil through metal detecting. Most objects discovered on ploughed fields have been removed from their original location. Ploughing over the centuries can disturb the tops of features such as pits and ditches and drag artefacts out of these features into the ploughsoil.

The exact location where an object is found and its relationship to other features and objects is of the utmost importance to an archaeologist. Ken's metal-detected finds from the ploughsoil give us information on their probable date and how and what they were made of, but the extra knowledge recovered from the excavations can tell us so much more not just about the coins but about the people who buried them on the hilltop. The Hallaton excavations enable us to draw conclusions about who the people were, what animals they revered, how their society was organised, even what they might have believed in, and how the coins were used and why they were buried.

Above: There were no obvious pits to contain the hoards and the shape of the coins suggests that they were originally placed in bags, long since rotted away in the ground. Without this archaeological context the coins would have only been able to give us limited information about how and why they were buried.

Ian Leins at the British Museum has spent many years studying the thousands of Hallaton coins. This unusually large excavated assemblage has enabled him to devise a new dating system for Corieltavian coins. The earliest coins have images but no inscriptions on them and are often quite worn, suggesting that they had been in circulation for some time. Later coins are inscribed with what are thought to be the names of tribal chieftains of the Corieltavi. Traditionally it was thought that each chieftain would have ruled for a number of years before giving way to the next, who would mint his own set of coins. Every hoard from Hallaton contains examples of all of the different names on unworn coins, so Ian concluded that the coins were deposited over a very short period of time (15–20 years). This makes it very likely that many of the different types of coins were produced at the same time – meaning that the chieftains named on the coins were also ruling at the same time. Instead of a single large East Midlands tribe with one chief, it seems much more likely that the Corieltavi were made up of various small groups, each with their own ruler, some of whom minted their own coinage. Based on Ian's work the Hallaton coins fall into three date ranges:

(3) AD 43–AD 50

Coin hoards deposited in the entranceway and with the helmet. This was the main phase of ritual deposition. The latest coin found was a Roman issue of Claudius dating to AD 41/2.

(1) 50 BC–1 BC

Gold coins deposited outside the shrine, possibly before the boundary ditch was dug. Twenty-five coins were found, most from the area immediately east of the entrance. These were probably from a single hoard disturbed by the subsequent burial of the animal bones. Along with a 1st-century BC brooch, they are the earliest identified ritual deposits on the site.

(2) Pre-conquest AD 30–AD 43

Coins were placed in the ditch alongside the bowl, ingots and other finds. These were mostly uninscribed.

Celtic Imagery

The first British coins

Coins first made their appearance on the near Continent from the end of the 4th century BC. Britain was the last part of the Celtic world to adopt its own coinage. Gold coins made by tribes in Gaul begin to circulate in the south and east of England in the 2nd century BC, but the earliest known British coins were 'potins' made from an alloy of copper and tin, which are mostly found in Kent. Gold coins were not made in Britain until the 1st century BC. The imported Gaulish coins strongly influenced the first British-made coins. Increasing contact with the Roman world from the later the 1st century BC led to designs on the coins, especially those of the tribes in southern Britain, becoming more Classical. Iron Age coins were produced in Britain right up to and probably just after the Roman invasion.

Most Corieltavian coins depict images of horses or boars, and nearly all of the Hallaton coins are decorated with horses. The imagery on British coins is copied from that found on coins from Gaul, which in turn had probably been copied from early Greek designs. One of the most imitated Greek coins is the gold stater of Philip II of Macedon (359–366 BC). As the coins were copied and re-copied, different artists added their own interpretations and the designs gradually became more stylised and individual.

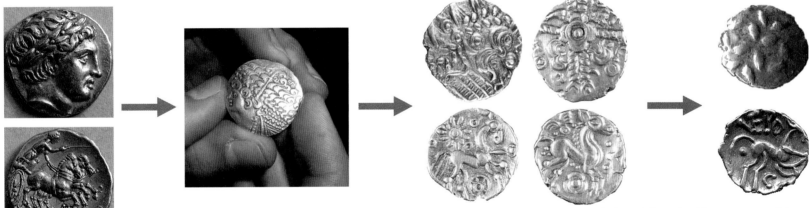

Above: The imagery on the Corieltavian coins is ultimately derived from the 4th century BC Philip II of Macedon stater (far left), which bears the head of the god Apollo wearing a wreath on one side and a two-horse chariot driven by a charioteer with a whip on the other. These coins had been introduced as a standardised way of paying armies and the idea of coins quickly spread as mercenaries returned home with their 'pay'. Gaulish copies still show the recognisable head of hair, laurel wreath and ear. By the 1st century BC, the head on the British gold coins from Hallaton has been transformed into stylised patterns although the laurel wreath is still recognisable. The chariot has become a single horse although a wheel is still there beneath the horse's body and the charioteer's whip has become patterns of pellets, suns and sometimes multiple tails. The 1st-century AD silver coins on the right still show the horse but by now the laurel wreath is almost unrecognisable. Hallaton coins at 150%.

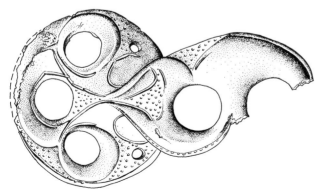

Left: Inspiration for the imagery on coins probably also came from decorated jewellery, silverware, ceramics and other objects. This drawing of the Iron Age tankard handle from Hallaton shows an asymmetric design, with circles, swirls and dot-filled triangles – all common themes in Celtic art. Drawing by Dave Hopkins. Length 80mm.

The Iron Age is known for its beautiful art, particularly metalwork. High quality iron ore was generally widely available and iron working occurred not just in villages but also possibly within larger specialised centres. Copper alloy objects were also made locally and many objects, such as horse gear, were elaborately decorated. Iron Age coins were no different. Celtic artwork is mostly based around highly stylised images of the natural world. The Corieltavian coins from Hallaton predominantly feature horses on one side with abstract decoration on the other. Although the image of the horse was derived from the chariot on the Macedonian coin, the horse also had a strong significance in the Iron Age world, and the style of the horses on the different coins from Hallaton is very varied. By the time of the Roman invasion many of the designs had transformed into patterns and stylised images virtually unrecognisable from the originals.

The horses on the early silver uninscribed coins have chunky, curved bodies but spindly, jointed legs with prominent circles for joints. Often the legs are exaggerated. The heads are simplistic and stylised with large curved ears and there is little other decoration.

The horses on the regional gold staters are very different to those on the silver coins. Instead of the outline of a curved body, swirling lines are used, which over time degenerate into crescent patterns. The legs also have dots for the joints. These are probably the least natural of the Corieltavian horses, with their strange triangular heads and large circular eye.

The inscribed silver coins depict a variety of horses and designs and these tend to be the most complicated, with suns, wheels, rings and dots added. The horse has a thin curving tail similar to that on the prehistoric White Horse at Uffington (Wiltshire). Considering the small size of the coins, the detail that the Iron Age artist managed to inscribe into the die to produce these miniature masterpieces is staggering.

Other tribes

The Hallaton hoards contained coins from every other coin-producing tribe in Britain except one (the Cantii from Kent), showing that there were contacts between Leicestershire and the south. Each group of coins had their own unique regional identity.

The Catuvellauni and Atrebates (tribes to the south) used more realistic and classical images on their later coins, possibly because they had more direct contact with the formalised designs of the Roman world.

This Dobunnic coin from Hallaton (*right*) is similar to the 1st-century BC British staters also found on the site (*left*), with donkey-like 'cartoon' horses and the laurel wreath, hair and eyes still recognisable on the obverse.

Making Iron Age Coins

Two different techniques were used for making coins: striking and casting. Cast coins are known to have been made in some regions, especially Kent. Molten metal was poured into moulds inscribed with designs. This produced a sheet of linked coins, which were then broken apart when cooled. However, most Iron Age coins, including those from Hallaton, were struck individually using blanks made in clay moulds.

The moulds were trays with circular depressions into which small pieces of cut metal were evenly distributed. The trays were then heated and the metal melted down into pellets of uniform weight and size. Once cooled, the pellets would be removed from the flan trays and hammered into a flat disc or 'flan'. These flans were reheated and struck between engraved dies to create coins. Two dies were used, a lower one for the obverse image, which was slightly concave to hold the flan in place, and an upper one for the reverse, which was placed over the top. The coin was then 'struck' with a single hammer blow, impressing the images on the dies into the soft metal of the flan, creating a dish-shaped coin. Most of the coins would have been 'hot struck' – that is, the blanks would be heated before striking. Experiments suggest that a team of eight to ten people could have produced about 450 coins an hour from ready-made blanks.

Considering the small size of some of the coins, the skill required to engrave the images and patterns on the dies must have been significant. They were the product of highly accomplished craftworkers, who doubtless guarded the 'mysteries' of their trade and were probably considered important people within the tribe. The actual striking of the coins was probably less skilled – many coins have been hit off-centre and the edges of the design are missing.

Where were the Hallaton coins made?

It seems likely that some coins were made in specialised centres. The coins of Cunobelin, for instance, have the letters CAMV on the reverse, short for Camulodunum (modern Colchester), which was probably where this chief's coins were minted.

No evidence was found at Hallaton to indicate that the coins were being made there. Thousands of coin mould fragments from Old Sleaford (Lincolnshire) suggest that this could have been a possible source. Three different sizes of moulds correspond to the three sizes of Corieltavian coins (stater, unit and half unit). However there is evidence for coin manufacture closer to home: mould fragments from Bath Lane in Leicester suggest that coins were made there in the late Iron Age.

Very few coin dies have been found, but they would have been made from metal and may not have survived in the archaeological record. Many of the Corieltavian coins have blank or very faint designs on the reverse suggesting that the dies had worn down and not been replaced.

Left: Replica Iron Age coins being struck at a Harborough Museum open day at Burrough Hill. Photograph courtesy of Hazel Wallace.

Right: The blank discs for the Hallaton coins would have been made in a clay mould like this one from Bath Lane, Leicester.

In the British Iron Age, coins were not used in the same way as today. They are more likely to have been symbols of wealth and prestige, and probably only the powerful and rich members of society would have had access to them. Coins, particularly in hoards, are often found away from settlements in areas thought to have religious or ritual significance; coins may have been considered 'special', with links to the gods that made them suitable for ritual offerings. Gold coins varied in colour from deep rose to bright yellow and different colours may have been regarded as more suitable for particular transactions.

Left: Corieltavian coins come in four distinct sizes. The largest, on the left, were the gold staters (around the same size as a modern penny). The silver unit (smaller than a 5p piece) was the most common coin found at Hallaton. Silver half units and minims were smaller still and often had similar designs to the units.

The lower image shows the dished profile created by the dies. Coins shown at 175%.
© Leicestershire County Council.

If the coins were not used as money then why were there different sizes? It may be that the manufacturers were copying the Romans, who needed coins of a standardised worth to pay their soldiers. Perhaps the size conveyed a value, so that different tribal coinages could be exchanged despite their varied designs. The introduction of coins into Iron Age society would have provided a convenient and visible way for high-ranking people to make gifts to their followers and to cement alliances and social contracts, even if they were rarely used for general trade and everyday transactions. Today we use money to acquire objects with fixed values or to create profit. In Iron Age societies using coins as gifts may have helped to consolidate relationships between different groups. By having their own coinage with recognisable designs and names, tribal leaders had a symbol of their authority that at the same time carried a monetary value.

It is not certain where the metal to make the coins came from. Gold could have been mined in Ireland or Wales, but it is more likely that the gold for the first British coins came from melting down Continental coins. Analysis of some of the Iron Age silver coins from Hallaton suggests that they were made from a very pure silver, debased with copper alloy. The silver bullion was probably imported from the Mediterranean world, perhaps coming from Roman silver mines in Spain. It might have come to Britain in the form of Roman silver coins, or as ingots or other objects. A silver ingot from Hallaton has two partially melted coins (probably local issues) still visible in the upper surface (*see page 44*). This might suggest that although most batches of local Iron Age coins were made using imported bullion, sometimes the coins themselves were melted down for re-use.

Britain's first forgeries?

Some of the coins found on site were made from copper and then plated with gold to make them look like solid gold. It seems that even as far back as the Iron Age people were forging coins, although it's not known whether this was a deliberate policy by the tribe or a rogue individual trying to pass off fakes as genuine gold coins. The Corieltavian gold staters on the right all have copper cores, but traces of gold plating show that when new they would have looked just like the real thing.

The Hallaton Helmet

Once the excitement of excavating the coin hoards had died down the team got busy cleaning up the rest of the site. Ken had been going over the newly opened areas with his metal detector and had identified a very strong signal on the edge of the ditch just south of the entrance. Excavation revealed a pit cut into the boundary ditch. As the archaeologists began to excavate, it soon became clear that there was at least one more large coin hoard, with fragments of metal next to it. Despite cleaning round the pieces of iron very carefully, neither the archaeologists nor the fieldworkers had any idea what it could be. Several pieces on the top looked silvery and jokes were made on site about one of the pieces looking like an ear. Back in the office, ULAS director Richard Buckley knew exactly what this was – the earguard from a Roman helmet. It was clear that this was a 'special' deposit.

The big group of coins was removed in the same way as the other hoards, but the helmet was a much larger deposit and after 2000 years in the ground was extremely fragile. It was decided that the only way to get it out of the ground without destroying it would be to try and consolidate the bits and lift it in one large block with the surrounding soil.

50mm

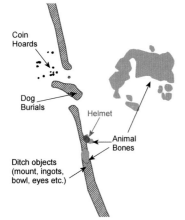

Coin
Hoards

Dog
Burials

Helmet

Animal
Bones

Ditch objects
(mount, ingots,
bowl, eyes etc.)

Above: The silver ear was initially the only object that indicated that the fragments of metal were in fact from a Roman helmet.

Right: Recording the helmet prior to it being lifted from the ground.

The helmet dates to the 1st century AD and it seems likely that it originally belonged to a Roman cavalry officer of very high rank. It was made of iron, covered in silver foil and ornately decorated. It was buried with over 1000 coins which date its deposition to around the time of the Roman invasion in AD 43, and is almost certainly a ritual offering made at broadly the same time as the entrance coin hoards. In the late Iron Age, ditches and pits were commonly used for the deposition of coins and other artefacts, but use of pits for deposition appears to decline during the Roman period. The pit's location was therefore probably very meaningful to the people who buried the helmet. It had been placed (probably deliberately) over an earlier pit full of pig bones and the helmet pit had disturbed some of the bones. These obviously meant something significant to the pit diggers as they had carefully collected them and reburied them with the helmet parts.

The location of the helmet mid-way along the eastern edge of the ditch may have reflected the need to create a link between the coin hoards, other objects buried in the ditch, and the animal bones outside. Perhaps the helmet and coins were also buried close to the guard dog in the ditch for added protection. The helmet bowl (the part that sits on the wearer's head) had been placed upside down in the ditch. Bones and coins had been carefully interleaved between several cheekpieces that were stacked against each other, next to the helmet bowl.

The helmet was probably buried with the coins as a gift to the gods – whether to secure protection from or to celebrate an alliance with the advancing Romans, or simply because it was valued as a high-status object with which to appease the gods – is unknown.

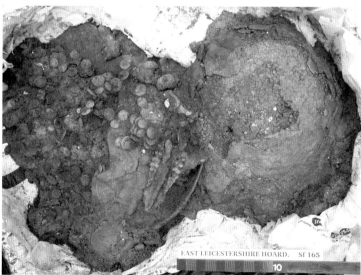

EAST LEICESTERSHIRE HOARD.   SF 165

Lifting the helmet

Graham Morgan, the conservator at the University of Leicester's School of Archaeology supervised the removal of the helmet block.

First the top of the pit was cleaned and recorded. Then a trench was carefully excavated all the way round the helmet, creating a free-standing plinth of soil with the helmet inside.

A barrier layer of wet tissue-paper, aluminium foil and cling film was then placed over the soil block to prevent the plaster from touching the objects and to act as a release when the helmet was later excavated.

Next, the whole block was carefully coated in layer after layer of plaster of Paris. Once dry the plaster formed a rigid container for the fragile helmet.

Finally, the block was undercut so the whole 'container' could be lifted out of the ground and turned over. The block was covered in black bin-bags to keep out the light and stored in a dry room until it could be taken to the British Museum for excavation and conservation.

Left: Several cheekpieces had been carefully stacked to one side of the helmet bowl and were interleaved with animal bone and coins. Note the supermarket carrier bag that had to be used when the conservators ran out of cling film!

Restoring the Helmet

The helmet has been conserved and painstakingly pieced together over a period of nearly a decade. By 2011 many hundreds of fragments had been removed from the soil block and consolidated. Each part then had to be identified before the helmet could be reconstructed. Marilyn Hockey at the British Museum has spent a large part of the last 10 years working on this delicate project.

To get a clearer picture of what lay buried in the soil, the blocks containing the helmet and the coins were first X-rayed. The dense clay and the iron of the helmet made it difficult to get a clear picture of exactly what was hidden in the soil, but the coins were easy to spot.

The helmet was too fragile to be turned the right way up, so Marilyn and the other British Museum conservators had to excavate the block in reverse order, from the bottom up. The soil was carefully removed in stages using fine tools, under magnification. Photographs were taken at every stage and each layer was plotted onto gridded paper. The process of removing the objects from the soil took over 300 hours.

Below: X-rays of two of the cheekpieces showed decoration that was not visible on the corroded iron surface (right), and revealed the presence of more coins and a packet of folded silver foil (left). © The Trustees of the British Museum.

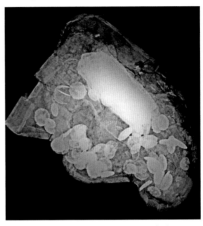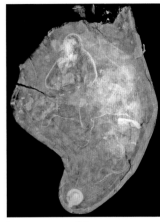

Left: The x-ray of one of the blocks from the helmet pit showing some of the coins.
Below: A few of the thousands of fragments of helmet waiting to be pieced together.
© The Trustees of the British Museum.

Most of the helmet fragments were in an extremely poor state of preservation. The iron core of the helmet had rusted away and the silver covering the iron had mineralised leaving only a paper-thin film. Initially it was feared that the pieces were too damaged to have any surviving detail of the decoration, but Marilyn's careful excavation soon revealed the first cheekpiece with much of its silver decoration still intact.

Over the years the block of soil has yielded many surprises. Initially it was thought that the pit contained a single Roman helmet, but it soon became apparent that there was more to the deposit. As well as the helmet bowl, there turned out to be a total of seven cheekpieces, instead of the two that would be expected. In addition, small bundles of folded silver foil were found. Could this silver have been removed from other perhaps damaged helmets for re-use in repairs?

Bent hinge pins were also found in the block. It seems that at least one of the cheekpieces was originally attached to the helmet – possibly the cheekpiece was forcibly removed before burial. Was the helmet deliberately 'killed' to remove it from the everyday world and make it more acceptable to the gods?

Above: This cheekpiece with a Roman (Emperor?) on horseback was the first to be uncovered. Photograph © Leicestershire County Council, courtesy of the British Museum.

Right: the restored helmet is the result of hundreds of hours of patient excavation and reconstruction by the team at the British Museum. Photographs © The Trustees of the British Museum.

Images of Rome

Even in its bad state of decay the cavalry helmet is one of the most elaborate ever discovered in north-west Europe, with decoration of a very high standard. It seems more likely to have been a ceremonial object worn by an officer for special occasions rather than in battle. Although the core of the helmet is made from iron, it would originally have been a very beautiful object, plated with silver and covered in relief decoration using the repoussé technique (where the design is hammered out from the inside), with elements of the decoration picked out in gold leaf. At least one of the seven cheekpieces (four right-hand and three left-hand) was originally attached to the helmet; various rivets of iron and copper alloy were also found.

The helmet bowl portrays a laurel wreath, the symbol of martial victory but there is no sign of the stylised hair decoration that is found on some other Roman helmets. The neck-guard has scrolled leaf patterns and the scalloped browguard bears a female bust at the centre.

The best preserved cheekpiece (from the left side) depicts a triumphant Roman figure on horseback, armoured but bare-headed, with his arm outstretched in a salute. Behind him flies a winged Victory holding a victor's palm-leaf. Below the horse's hooves sits a figure symbolising defeat, with their hands clasped to their head next to an abandoned shield and helmet. A second near-complete cheekpiece also shows a mounted rider and Victory, this time holding a laurel crown. These are both representations of the military power of Rome 'lording it' over a defeated people. Other cheek-pieces are awaiting reconstruction at the British Museum. Three show images of mounted horsemen, another shows a shield and helmet at its edge but is very fragmentary.

Left: The reconstructed helmet from Hallaton is on display in Harborough Museum. Right: An artist's reconstruction of what it might have looked like when new. Drawing by Bob Whale, © Leicestershire County Council.

The face of an Emperor?

Who is the victorious bare-headed rider on horseback shown on the cheekpiece? It almost certainly represents a Roman person of high status, possibly an Emperor. Suggestions from various experts range from Claudius, to Tiberius, Nero or even Caligula.

A defeated people?

The cheekpieces are decorated with scenes of Roman victory. The crouched figure beneath what may be a Roman Emperor, next to an abandoned shield and helmet is the ultimate defining image of a conquered and defeated people.

This is a common scene in Roman iconography and probably represents the defeat of a tribal people by the Romans. Whether the scene celebrates a particular Roman victory is not known.

There is some debate as to whether the figure on the left is male or female. Some experts think that the clothing indicates a lady and it has even been suggested that this could be one of the first visual representations of Britannia with her plumed helmet and shield.

© Leicestershire County Council.

One of the most impressive features of the helmet is the elaborate scalloped brow-guard (*right*), with its sweeping swags and cabling around the edge. This is dominated by a female bust flanked by two lions, with their forepaws resting on another animal. Unfortunately much of the female head is damaged so it is hard to say exactly who is depicted. Suggestions include Cybele, the mother goddess, known in Rome as Magna Mater (Great Mother). Her association with victory would make her a perfect choice for a Roman helmet.

Below: Although most of the cheekpieces seem to show similar images of victorious Roman Emperors, one is very different. Although still undergoing conservation, X-rays have revealed a face near the top that looks decidedly un-Roman. The face is in profile and seems to have a beard and some kind of head covering. At his feet lie a Roman helmet (looking quite similar to the Hallaton helmet), a shield and a cornucopia (horn of plenty).

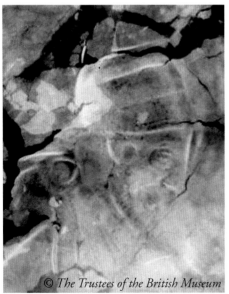

Military items are often found in ritual deposits in Iron Age and Roman Gaul. One of the two Roman helmets found in the River Waal in Nijmegen, Netherlands, was associated with additional cheekpieces. Six helmets from the Kops Plateau, also in Nijmegen, were buried in shallow pits in what is thought to be a ritual context along with smashed pottery and possibly the remains of food and drink. The silver foil had been removed from two of the facemasks, reminiscent of the small packets of silver foil found from Hallaton. Seven iron cheekpieces and body armour fragments buried in a ditch at Hofstad, Netherlands, and dating to the period AD 40–100 might also provide a parallel for Hallaton.

Closer to Hallaton, decorated helmet cheekpieces have been found at found at Brough (Nottinghamshire) and in Leicester. The 3rd-century AD Guisborough helmet had been folded and carefully arranged in a bed of gravel away from any Roman site, possibly suggesting a ritual context. The recently discovered Crosby Garret helmet, thought to have been the prized possession of an auxiliary serving in a Roman cavalry regiment on the northern frontier in the 2nd century AD, had also been folded before burial.

Above: The Hallaton helmet is not the only one from the area. This bronze cheekpiece and earguard, now at the Jewry Wall Museum, was found near Bath Lane, in Leicester.

What was the helmet doing at Hallaton?

How the helmet parts came to be buried on a native British ritual site on a hilltop in rural Leicestershire at about the same time as the Roman invasion is one of the most puzzling questions raised by the site. Although helmets do not seem to be common objects in later Iron Age Britain, there are a number of British coins with images of helmets on them. A Roman style helmet is shown on one of Cunobelin's later coins suggesting that high-quality Roman helmets similar to the one found at Hallaton might have been known (and worn) in Britain before the conquest. Exactly how the local inhabitants would have got hold of such a magnificent helmet and the cheekpieces is a mystery. Several explanations are possible:

 The helmet could have been brought to Hallaton by a local man who had served in the Roman army. The Romans often recruited skilled soldiers and horsemen from local tribes and there are indications that high-ranking Britons in the south sent their sons to be trained in the Roman army. On the Continent, local warriors who were recruited into the Roman army sometimes buried their armour and helmets and weapons, often in rivers or boggy places during coming of age rituals. Older men coming to the end of their service might also bury their military kit. It is possible that Roman troops were present in Britain for some time before AD 43, and that (like the Gauls) Britons might have fought both against and with Roman troops. Young men may have joined the Roman army as auxiliary cavalryman on the Continent and returned home bringing back not only the helmets themselves but perhaps also the habit of burying them as an offering to the gods. However, this does not explain the extra cheekpieces and silver foil.

 The helmet could have been brought to Leicestershire by the Romans. It might have been gifted to a local chieftain to ease the Roman army's passage through the area and to avoid having to fight the locals. Diplomatic gifts were often used by the Romans to gain allies in the lands they invaded. The shrine overlooks the Roman road to Leicester and lies near the junction of two other important routes and could have been a strategic location for the Romans in their move northwards. The Roman small town of Medbourne lies 2.5 miles to the south-east and there is a Roman marching camp at Weston by Welland across the river valley to the south. Recent excavations there suggest that Iron Age Britons occupied the hilltop at about the same time as the shrine was in use and a small group of six Iron Age coins buried in the base of a burnt feature perhaps mirrors the ritual activity at Hallaton. Leicester, just 15 miles to the north-west, was a significant late Iron Age settlement which was chosen to be the Roman *civitas* capital for the area – the Hallaton helmet could be a gift to a leader from the Leicester area, who facilitated the Roman invasion, and was perhaps even one of the eleven tribal chieftains who surrendered to Claudius.

 The local tribe could have taken the helmet and other pieces from the Roman army during a skirmish or battle. The camp at Weston by Welland shows the Roman army was close by. The various helmet pieces might have been carried by the army as 'spares' to mend and repair other helmets. This would explain the odd fragments and the folded silver foil. Some coin experts have suggested that a new type of coin from Hallaton represents the only known coinage of Togodumnus, struck around the time of the AD 43 Roman landings. Conceivably Hallaton was an assembly point for the British armies that opposed the Romans after the Claudian invasion.

© Leicestershire County Council.

Offerings in the Ditch

By the end of 2003 most of the ritual area had been uncovered and excavated. The third season was intended to be a small-scale operation funded by ULAS and using volunteers from the HFWG to hand dig three small trenches. The objective was to look in more detail at some of the pits containing animal bone which had not been previously been excavated. At Easter 2005 a trench was opened to examine one pit that overlay the boundary ditch.

Conditions on site were truly awful and the team worked in driving winds, rain and even sleet. It was clear that a sump was needed to drain the water from the area that the archaeologists wanted to work on. The trench was extended and it was decided to dig a section through the ditch, where it had already been damaged by a later plough furrow and a land drain. Once the top of the drain had been exposed, however, Ken started to get signals on his metal detector and the excavation slowed to recover the finds properly. Sure enough several coins were recovered – this was unusual, as hardly anything had been found in the rest of the ditch. Ken then got what he described as a 'big' signal and careful trowelling revealed the first of the objects – a decorated silver disc with broken edges, and a handful of coins. Following this discovery, and with Ken still getting loud signals from the detector, the land drain was removed. Excavation of this section of the ditch revealed yet more artefacts, including two ingots, a silver bowl, gold foil, and blue and white glass fragments, all within a space of just 25–30cm.

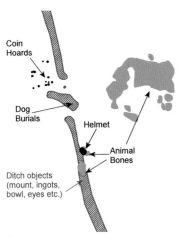

In 2005 the team were forced to work in some dreadful weather conditions. Their dedication paid off when a deposit of metalwork was found in the ditch.

Right: the section of ditch that was removed to act as a sump for the pit (the darker area in the foreground), just before the removal of the land drain and the discovery of the objects.

Above: The objects from the boundary ditch as they were revealed in excavation. The semi-circular ingot (left) had been placed upright against the eastern side of the ditch. The silver bowl and triangular ingot (centre) had also been placed on their sides, this time in the middle of the ditch. The bowl lay almost directly below the land drain – the slot in the side of it may have been made by the workers who laid the field drains. The decorated silver disc (right) had been placed face down in the upper fill of the ditch.

Below: The bowl and the two ingots as they were lifted from the mud.

The silver bowl

This beautiful 2,000-year-old hand-made silver bowl is one of the earliest known examples from Britain and provides new evidence on the traditions of the Iron Age silversmith. Work undertaken by the London Assay Office on the composition of the silver has determined that the 109mm diameter bowl was high in silver (84%), debased with relatively pure copper (13%). The rest of the alloy consisted of small amounts of gold, lead, and tin. Pure silver is an extremely soft metal, so copper is added to make it harder. Roman silversmiths tended to debase their silver with about 1–5% copper to produce silver vessels. The addition of around 13% copper would have resulted in a harder and more durable alloy, but one that would still be soft enough to be worked. The choice of this particular alloy for the bowl suggests that the metalworker who made it was quite experienced, but not working in the Roman tradition. The alloy would seem to have been deliberately created by a skilled British metalworker specifically to make this bowl. Careful study of the bowl by modern silversmiths suggests that the techniques used then were very similar to those still used today. A cache of iron hammers found at Fiskerton (Lincolnshire) closely resemble modern metalworking tools. Silver working may have been a more common practice in Iron Age Britain than previously realised.

The Hallaton bowl is well made and the silversmith was certainly a skilled craftworker – this was clearly not a first attempt at making such an object. The presence of silver objects in other hoards and on ritual sites has led archaeologists to believe that silver may sometimes have been used specifically for ritual purposes at this time (as opposed to earlier periods when bronze and gold were favoured).

The cut in the base of the bowl was certainly made in antiquity. However the soil around the cut and the state of the edges suggest that this may have been a slip of the spade of the person digging the land drain, rather than a deliberate act of mutilation to 'kill' the object before it was buried. Tiny central marks on both the inside and outside, which were made by turning a pair of dividers, and the slightly crude finish of the outer surface might suggest that the bowl was unfinished, or that what we might see as a 'perfect' surface was not required.

The bowl has few close parallels. A copper alloy bowl of similar size thought to be from the Melsonby hoard (North Yorkshire) has a similar date in the early or mid 1st century AD. Fragments of a small silver vessel similar to the Hallaton bowl were recovered from Snettisham (Norfolk), where a coin hoard stolen by Nighthawks is said to have been buried in a silver bowl.

Above right: The Hallaton silver bowl is one of the earliest known examples of British silversmithing recovered from an archaeological context.
Right: The outer surface of the bowl was left slightly rough and not polished smooth. The cut in the base was probably made when the land drain was inserted above it. Scale in cm.
Photographs © Leicestershire County Council, courtesy of Harborough Museum.

 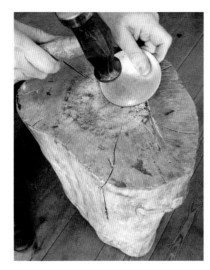  

Recreating the Hallaton bowl

As part of an exhibition at the Goldsmiths Hall, London, silversmith Alex Brogden created a replica silver bowl using similar manufacturing techniques to those used in the Iron Age. Two main methods are used to create rounded objects. 'Raising' involves hammering a flat disc over a hard rounded former creating a uniform thickness. The uneven profile of the Hallaton bowl, however, suggests that it was 'peened' – a simple method where the curved bowl is formed by hammering a silver disc into a depression. Surprisingly the whole process of creating the bowl took just half a day.

Above (L–R): A flat disc of silver is prepared by marking the centre and using compasses to mark out the circle. The bowl shape is created by hammering into a depression in a block of wood. A harder surface is then used to create the curve of the bowl using a round hammer to achieve the desired depth and shape.

Below: The edge of the bowl is hammered down to form the lip, then the bowl is heated before being planished over a 'stake' to smooth out the bumps. The stake used for the Hallaton bowl appears to have had a small cut mark on it, creating tiny raised lines on the inside of the bowl. Below right: Silversmith Alex Brogden with the finished replica, which took less than a day to make.

The ingots

The two ingots recovered from the ditch were both very different. The semi-circular ingot is 189mm in length and weighs 913.8g. It is made from tin bronze (approximately 85% copper and 13% tin). It was cast in a semi-circular mould and is flat on one side and slightly curved on the other, with a small casting sprue shaped like a rounded knob at the top. Although ingots are known in many forms in the Iron Age, the plano-convex shape (like a lens) was the most common and continued to be made into the Roman period.

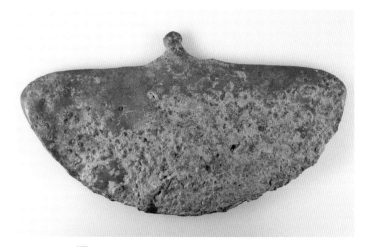

The triangular ingot is *c.* 115mm long and weighs 1247.8g. It is made of silver and appears to be from the base of a crucible. In order to turn ingots into objects, the metal had to be re-melted. This would have been done in a ceramic crucible. Typically, Iron Age crucibles in Britain were triangular, and the silver ingot is the same size and shape as a large triangular crucible. The metal appears to come at least in part from melted down local coins (two coins are just visible on the surface) although why the silver from the base of the crucible was not used to make anything is not known. Ingots were a convenient way of storing metal until it was ready to be turned into objects.

The decorated mount

The silver circular mount was the first object found in the ditch, surrounded by silver coins. It was originally *c.* 85mm across, and bears relief decoration with a central eight-petalled pattern, inside several circles. Traces of gilt suggest that the decoration was originally picked out in gold. Dots, circles and spirals are common motifs on Iron Age objects, but this pattern seems more Roman than Celtic. It does resemble Roman horse harness mounts or decoration perhaps attached to armour, although there are no attachments on the back.

melted coins

Much of the original outer edge had been badly broken, but despite this, replacement holes had been made along the new edge. Given that the damage was likely to have ruined its visual appeal, the disc must have held some other value. The owner may have had a personal attachment to it – perhaps it was a family item passed down through the generations or had some other meaning that is lost to us today.

Above right: The two ingots. The semi-circular ingot is made of tin bronze, while the triangular ingot weighs 2kg and is made from melting silver coins, two of which can still be seen sticking out, near the bottom corner. Left: The silver mount with traces of gilt still remaining on the decoration.
Photographs © Leicestershire County Council.

The 'eyes'

Pieces of blue and white glass were found in dark soil in the bottom of the ditch, along with tiny fragments of thin gold foil. When reconstructed the glass formed two blue circular objects approximately 14mm wide with white 'collars', domed on one side and flat on the other, giving the impression of eyes. Chemical analysis of the glass suggests that they are Roman, produced with natron and coloured by adding manganese and cobalt. On the back of the 'eyes' is birch bark tar with a textured surface. Birch bark tar is used as a glue and the 'eyes' may originally have been attached to another, long since disintegrated object, such as wood. Both the materials and the tar are consistent with a 1st-century AD date. The decomposition of a wooden object might also explain the dark colour of the soil found in the base of the ditch.

The 'eyes' may be from a gilded wooden head or figurine, such as an idol. Human heads are a common feature in late Iron Age art, but the eyes tend to be lentoid rather than round. Other contemporary examples of eyes made from a different material to the head include the bronze head of a woman from Silkstead (Hampshire), which has round pebbles for eyes, and an animal-hoofed bronze figure dredged from the river at Bouray, Essonne (France), which has one remaining circular blue and white eye similar to the Hallaton glass. Iron Age wooden idols in the shape of human figures are known from both Britain and Ireland, and wooden carvings of animals are also common, although the few known examples with glass or pebble eyes tend to be found on stone or metal sculptures.

Examples of statues with prominent eyes include this replica of the Celtic head from Mšecké Žehrovice, Czech Republic (above left). A hollow bronze head of a girl from Silkstead (above right), dating to the 1st or 2nd century AD has black pebbles for eyes. Photo by John Crook, © Winchester City Council Museums Service.

The reconstructed glass fragments look like eyes and could have been glued to a wooden idol using birch bark tar, some of which is still visible on the back of the fragments.
© Leicestershire County Council (above) & The Trustees of the British Museum (right).

Libation and offerings

The collection of objects in the ditch is dated by the accompanying 139 coins to the early 1st century AD. As most of the coins are the earlier uninscribed types, the artefacts were probably buried in the AD 30s, before the coin hoards and helmets were deposited above them in the edge of the same ditch.

Why was this small mixed group of objects buried here? Whatever significance they held individually, it is obvious that their deposition as a group was important, with each item being carefully positioned and interleaved with scatters of coins during the infilling of this section of the boundary ditch. There seems to be no strong common theme to link them together other than the coins and the fact that most of the items are silver in colour

It may be – as with the coin hoards, which each contained almost all of the major types of Corieltavian coins – that each object represents an offering from an individual person or group, which were assembled together as a communal deposit. The presence of dog bones in the ditch just to the north suggests that these objects required the same protection as the coin hoards.

The burial of the objects could perhaps have been part of a purification ritual to consecrate the site. The bowl was ideally suited to drinking from and could have been used for libations to the gods during the ceremonies enacted at Hallaton. The objects may also have been buried to mark the significance of this part of the newly backfilled ditch.

The Hallaton Pigs

One of the main reasons that Ken had decided to metal detect this field was the animal bones that had been picked up during the fieldwalking. The source of the animal bones became apparent as soon as the excavations began – an area approximately 12m square, east of the entrance, was strewn with fragments of bone. At first the archaeologists feared they might have stumbled across a group of farm burials. However as more and more bones were uncovered, all of them identified as pig, it became obvious that this was an unusual deposit related to the shrine. The dry weather in 2003 and the clayey soil made it very hard to see any features and trowelling was difficult. One afternoon Hazel returned to site with a kitchen broom to clean the surface.

'As we swept more and more bones were being revealed,' she remembers. 'When we had finished sweeping, the site appeared to be paved with bones.'

With such a large area to cover and so many bones, it was clear that the team couldn't excavate the whole deposit. The soil conditions made removing the already fragile bones very difficult, so a new strategy was developed. A grid was laid out over the area and about a quarter was sampled by collecting all of the soil and the bones in sample bags labelled with the findspot, and then transported back to the laboratory. The soil and bones were then washed through sieves to make sure that all of the bone and any other artefacts were collected.

Below the top layer of bone, several pits began to appear. The bones in these pits were not as fragmented as in the layer above, with some clearly articulated remains. It appeared that pig body parts had been placed in the pits – perhaps as offerings to the gods. The fragmented bone spread over the top might be a midden of discarded bones from the remnants of a feast.

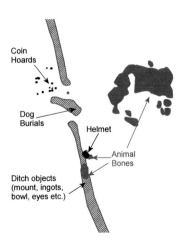

Other groups of pig bone were found near where the helmet was buried and in another pit overlying the ditch, close to where the silver bowl and other objects were discovered.

Above right: Members of the HFWG cleaning the spread of bones east of the entranceway.

Right: As the loose dry soil was brushed away a veritable 'pavement of bones' was revealed.

Ken used his detector routinely to warn the excavators when and where they should expect metal. Detecting over the top of the animal bone pits produced a flurry of signals. Soon the team were digging up more coins, older and very different to the silver coins from the hoards. These were British coins, all made of gold and older than the Corieltavian coins. Twenty-five coins were found scattered across the area of the animal bones and it seems likely that these were part of what may have been the very first hoard buried on the site some 50–100 years before the rest of the coin hoards and other deposits. Another strong signal in the top of the bone deposits located a curious patterned copper object that turned out to be the handle from an Iron Age tankard.

Ken detecting the animal bone area, where gold coins and a copper alloy tankard handle were found. Coins shown at 200%.

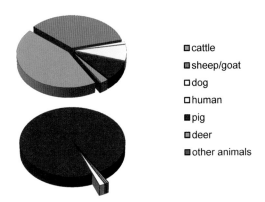

Above: Charts showing the typical range of animal bones from an Iron Age settlement site at Humberstone, Leicester (top) and from Hallaton (below).

Below: Pits containing articulated remains suggest that parts of pigs were placed in the pits as offerings to the gods. Scale 50cm.

Pigs are often found on Iron Age sites, but settlements tend to have a mixture of domesticated animals. Cattle and sheep are usually the most common, followed by pigs and other animals. The animal bones from Hallaton – where over 97% of the bones from the whole site were pig – is in marked contrast to most settlements and emphasises the unusual nature of the site. The remaining 3% of the bones includes the dogs, human bone and a handful of other animal bones.

The remains of about 80 individual pigs were excavated from the pits. Given that less than a quarter of the area was dug, there could be more than 300 pigs buried on the hilltop. They were predominantly very young when they were killed (the average age of death was between 7–14 months). Pigs were normally slaughtered for their meat between the ages of 2–3 years, when they were well grown but the meat was still tender. The death of so many young animals would represent a big economic loss to the community and suggests that they were killed for reasons other than for everyday consumption.

Human bone

Pieces of human bone are commonly found on Iron Age sites. It is thought that this is the result of excarnation, where dead bodies were left on special platforms, for the flesh to rot and decay before the bones were collected up and buried. This is likely to have resulted in small bones being lost either by falling through gaps in the platform or by being carried off by the wind or scavengers. This may explain how bone fragments could end up in rubbish pits and on middens. At Hallaton only two joining fragments of human bone, from a humerus (upper arm), were found. These are unlikely to have got there by accident and may have been deliberately buried in the ditch and subsequently dug up during the burial of the helmet and reburied in amongst the helmet parts and coins.

The missing legs

When the animal bones were studied in detail patterns began to emerge. All parts of the pig skeleton were present, suggesting that the animals had been brought onto the site whole, before being divided up and placed in the pits. Strangely, though, there were far fewer examples of the right foreleg than expected. This pattern was consistent across every deposit containing pig bones that was looked at, with 80% of the pigs apparently missing their right front leg. The deliberate selection of particular parts of a skeleton often occurs on ritual sites, and a preference for a particular side is also common. Why the right front leg was chosen for special treatment is not known, although this theme is mirrored on other ritual sites. At the Romano-British shrine at Great Chesterford, right forelimbs were preferred, and the right forequarters of pigs were more common than left at the late prehistoric midden site at Llanmaes (south Wales), which contained thousands of pig bones. In ancient Greek and Roman animal sacrifices, right legs were considered to belong to the priest, while left legs were reserved for the gods or the underworld.

The significance of the right forelimbs and the reason for their exclusion from the pits at Hallaton remains unknown. Perhaps they were used as part of a special ritual and deposited elsewhere? There are still many unexcavated pits containing animal bone on the site, one of which could be full of the missing legs!

Animals and ritual

The ritual offering of animals was widespread in Iron Age and Roman Britain, with animal sacrifices and votive offerings often placed in graves and in pits on settlements. Special deposits of animal bone are also common at temples, where animals of a particular type and age were often chosen for burial. At the Romano-Celtic temple at Harlow over 80% of the identified bones were sheep, mostly lamb, and at Uley temple sheep/goat were also preferred, making up over 84% of the animal bones. Pigs were the animal of choice at the Roman temple at Chanctonbury Ring and at least 90% of the Iron Age bones from High Pasture Cave on the Isle of Skye were from pigs.

The importance of the pig bones is evident in other deposits from Hallaton. The pit containing the helmet had been dug into an existing pit full of pig bones, some of which had been carefully removed and re-buried in between the cheekpieces. Perhaps the incorporation of the bones created a link with the earlier deposits of animal bone, or maybe the bones were replaced there to appease the gods for disturbing the original offerings.

Above: Iron Age pigs probably looked like this Tamworth breed. Photograph © Whitelands Farm.

Right: Pig bones dug up from an earlier deposit were reburied with the helmet suggesting that the bones had a particular significance. The pig jaw and rib had been carefully placed in between the cheekpieces along with coins. Photograph courtesy of the Trustees of the British Museum.

Feasting and Sacrifice

The mass offerings of pig bones seem to fall into two categories. The placing of carefully selected portions of animals suggests some form of ritual sacrifice and offerings to the gods (known as 'chthonic' sacrifice), while the large quantities of bone over the pits could be the remains of feasting. Although the pits lie outside the shrine, they are immediately adjacent to the entrance and opposite the coin hoards. Pigs and coins face one another on opposite sides of the entranceway and were probably linked by shared ritual practices. The people offering up the pigs are likely to have been visible from inside the sacred space and vice versa. While coins were probably only owned by people of high status, access to pigs is likely to have been much more commonplace. The burial of coins and metalwork may have been restricted to certain individuals or groups (chieftains or priests perhaps) but participation in offerings of animals and feasting outside the boundary could have been a communal event open to everyone. In the same way that coins might represent wealth and the giving up of something of value to the gods for a chieftain, the loss of a pig could represent the sacrifice of something of equal value for an ordinary family. The offerings may have been followed by ritual feasting. Feasting was an important part of Iron Age life and would have brought together people from scattered communities, and helped to build relationships and alliances within the tribal group.

Butchery and cooking

Were the pigs cut up and cooked as part of a feast? There are very few signs of butchery on the Hallaton bones, but such traces are often hard to detect. Knives rather than cleavers seem to have been used in the Iron Age, and skilled butchers would know where best to cut through the muscles and sinews without leaving marks on the bone. Evidence for cooking is also difficult to identify – methods such as boiling would not necessarily leave any traces on the bones. No signs of any fires or of cooking pots were found during the excavations, although it is possible that the animals were butchered and cooked elsewhere and the animal parts brought to the ritual area for burial and feasting.

The tankard handle

The decorated copper alloy handle found amongst the animal bones belonged to an Iron Age tankard. Made of wood and held together with bands of bronze (some of which were also found) this large vessel would have had one, or possibly two handles attached by small rivets.

Tankards date from the 1st century BC and continued to be used after the Roman conquest. The association of tankards with the drinking of beer (Celtic *cervesia*) or mead, and their discovery in ritual contexts and with burials on a wide variety of sites suggests that they were used for special occasions or ceremonies

Left: the copper alloy tankard handle is curved and decorated with spirals and dots, similar in design to other handles found on ritual sites. © Leicestershire County Council.

Above: Iron Age tankards were large wooden or metal cups with one or two handles, like this replica based on the handle and strips of copper alloy found at Hallaton. Given their size and the amount of liquid they could hold, these vessels may have been passed from person to person at communal gatherings as part of a feasting ritual. © Leicestershire County Council.

Community feasts

A feast has always been a special meal, set apart from everyday activities. Feasting in the Iron Age was an opportunity to display wealth and power, to impress fellow chieftains or followers and potential new allies, to mark celebrations, trade and alliances, as well as to honour the gods. The eating of young animals and the presence of special items such as tankards could be seen as signs of particular 'luxury' reflecting high status.

In Celtic mythology pigs were associated with feasting and surviving accounts of Celtic customs emphasize the importance of seasonal feasts. Iron Age pigs are likely to have been similar to wild boar, which mate in the autumn with their young born in the following spring. Most of the pigs at Hallaton were killed before they were one year old and were probably culled during the autumn or winter months. This is similar to animal sacrifices at other shrines: the sheep offerings at Harlow and Uley are thought to represent autumn–winter sacrifices. At Danebury hillfort, propitiatory offerings in grain storage pits seem to have been made twice a year, perhaps coinciding with the festivals of *Beltane*, marking the start of summer and *Samhain* after the harvest in the late autumn (*see page 54*).

The large numbers of pigs at Hallaton indicate a sizable gathering. Three hundred pigs could feed 2000 people. Assuming that the feasts took place at the same time as the coin hoards, over some 15–20 years, the site could perhaps have hosted over a hundred people at a time for an annual gathering. Pigs were used purely for food, unlike other animals that provide secondary products while they are alive (e.g. wool from sheep) and the sacrifice of such a large number of young animals before they had reached their optimum age for slaughter would have represented a significant loss to the community.

© Leicestershire County Council.

An annual gathering and feast would have been a way of drawing together groups of people who would normally have been separated by distance. The period of time around the Roman invasion would have been one of uncertainty and fear and perhaps this was a way of appealing to the gods while at the same time drawing the community together.

Pigs and the Corieltavi

Pigs and boars were an important food source in Iron Age Britain and are likely to have been maintained as herds, particularly in wooded landscapes. The area around Hallaton is thought to have been at least partly wooded at this time. They might perhaps also have fed on waste from the settlement.

Above: The Rothwell Boar. Image courtesy of The Collection: Art and Archaeology in Lincolnshire.

However, pigs are also known to have a particular significance to Iron Age people. In Gaul, the boar was seen as a symbol of courage in war and of military prowess, and pork was the food of champions and warriors. Pigs were frequently buried in graves together with carts, weapons and decorated artefacts, suggesting that they were associated with people of high status.

Boars and pigs seem to have held a particular significance to the people of the East Midlands; their image was depicted on many objects found within what became the territory of the Corieltavi. The earliest gold and silver coins carried the image of a boar complete with prominent dorsal bristles (although hardly any of the Hallaton coins were of this type). An Iron Age shield thought to be a ritual deposit, dredged from the River Witham near Lincoln in the 19th century, had the image of a stylised boar on it. An Iron Age figure of a boar, made around the 1st century AD, was also found at Rothwell in Lincolnshire (*above*). It seems that the boar was a potent symbol of the Corieltavi, and might even have been their tribal emblem. Were pigs deliberately chosen for

 sacrifice because of their significance to the Iron Age inhabitants of this area? Given their predominance over other animals at Hallaton, this seems likely.

Above and right: Some Corieltavian coins have images of boars on them.

The Hallaton Shrine

So what was the site at Hallaton? Archaeologists often argue over exactly what constitutes ritual, but the fact that so many coins, other rare objects and animal bones were all carefully buried on this hilltop leaves little doubt that this was a ritual site. This was evidently a special place for small groups of people to gather as part of a larger tribal community, a place to come together to worship the gods and ask for favours in return for the offering of special gifts. The site is also close to the border with the southern Catuvellauni tribe, and the shrine and its rituals may have been be a way of expressing Corieltavian identity, a means of displaying power and status to the neighbouring tribe.

Other Iron Age shrines are known in Britain but most lie in the south of England and are associated with a building of some sort. These were usually square timber buildings (although others were circular) and were often surrounded by a *temenos* or sacred enclosure. Many were located within or close to settlements, presumably to serve the local population. However, classical sources also describe British Celtic deities as being worshipped in wild, natural places beneath the open sky or in sacred woods and groves. Prehistoric Britons evidently believed that they could communicate with their gods in such places. This may also explain why so few sites have been identified – a shrine in a natural groves or open spaces would leave little evidence for archaeologists to find.

The Hallaton shrine sits on the crest of a low hill looking out over the Welland valley to the south and appears to be a combination of the two types, an open air shrine, marked by a boundary ditch and palisade but without any formal building. It has some elements of the formal structure of a temple, with a defining boundary and entrance, and clearly marked zones for the burial of particular types of objects – but lies within a natural, open setting.

The hilltop may already have been sacred to the local people before the Iron Age: a possible Bronze Age burial mound was revealed by the geophysical survey and finds of Bronze Age metalwork suggest that the Iron Age people who found them must have kept them as they felt that they represented an important link with the past.

Above: Aerial view looking west towards the site showing its position on the crest of the hill above the village. Photograph courtesy of Chris Royall.

Left: View looking south across the Welland valley from the site.

Very little archaeological evidence was found within the interior of the shrine. Of course natural features such as stones and trees, or wooden objects such as statues or idols would not necessarily have left traces behind. The first century AD Roman poet Lucan describes a sacred grove in southern Gaul:

© Leicestershire County Council.

'A grove there was untouched by men's hands from ancient times, whose interlacing boughs enclosed a space of darkness and cold shade, and banished the sunlight from above ... gods were worshipped there with savage rites, the altars were heaped with hideous offerings, and every tree was sprinkled with human gore. On those boughs ... birds feared to perch; in those coverts, wild beasts would not lie down; no wind ever bore down upon that wood, nor thunderbolt hurled from black clouds; the trees, even when they spread their leaves to no breeze, rustled of themselves. Water, also, fell there in abundance from dark springs. The images of the gods grim and rude were uncouth blocks formed of felled tree-trunks. Their mere antiquity and the ghastly hue of the rotten timber struck terror. ... Legend also told that often the subterranean hollows quaked and bellowed, that yew trees fell down and rose again, that the glare of conflagrations came from trees that were not on fire, and that serpents twined and glided round their stems. The people never resorted thither to worship at close quarters, but left the place to the gods. For, when the sun is in mid-heaven or dark night fills the sky, the priest himself dreads their approach and fears to surprise the lord of the grove.'

Although Hallaton is so far unique in Britain it seems unlikely that this was the only site of its kind. There are many instances where hoards and special objects have been found in apparent isolation that could represent offerings in natural locations. The eight hundred plus East Anglian coins from Wickham Market (Suffolk) deposited in the earlier 1st century AD in a broken pot close to the boundary of an enclosure is one such example, but there are numerous others including the 1st-century BC Iron Age gold coins found in a cow's leg bone at Sedgeford (Norfolk), a hoard of gold torcs and brooches from Winchester, and the famous site at Snettisham (Norfolk), where twelve separate pits spread over three acres contained dozens of gold, electrum, silver and bronze torcs. Despite an intensive search, no evidence has ever been found for a temple or building. In an interesting parallel to Hallaton, a hoard of coins in a silver bowl and several ingots were rumoured to have been stolen from the site by Nighthawks. The work at Hallaton suggests that if we cared to look beyond the treasure itself and carried out proper archaeological investigations, we could be rewarded with a better understanding of how and why such objects were buried.

Gods & Beliefs

The popular image of Celtic shrines and religion usually involves a white-robed, long-haired Druid, leaning on an oak tree with sprigs of mistletoe in his hands. Classical writers such as Tacitus conjure up a less peaceful image, describing groves devoted to barbarous superstitions with 'altars drenched in the blood of prisoners' while the druids consulted their gods by reading human entrails. Julius Caesar suggests that Druids were held in great respect, acted as judges and had the power to excommunicate people from religious festivals, making them social outcasts. The Druids were exempt from taxes and military service and were equal in status to warrior nobles and were probably feared by most ordinary people. While there is no evidence that Druids were present at Hallaton, the layout of the site suggests that access was restricted to those who presided over the rituals and the offerings within the shrine.

The finds from Hallaton conjure up an image of a hilltop shrine, open to the air, with rituals including the burial of coins and metalwork on one side of the boundary carefully watched over by guard dogs, and the sacrifice of pigs and ritual feasting on the other side. We can imagine a special place where people from distant settlements would congregate on a regular basis to celebrate and make offerings. Experts think that the fourteen coin hoards and the helmet hoard were buried over about fifteen to twenty years, which would suggest an annual celebration. The pigs were all killed at the same time of year, suggesting a festival in the autumn or winter.

Although we know the names of several hundred Celtic gods, these are all derived from foreign writers and inscriptions. Iron Age Britons were predominantly farmers and would have been concerned with the cycles of the seasons and nature, and the fertility of the land and their animals. It seems likely that any festivals and offerings to the gods would have been connected to these fundamental themes. Following the autumn harvest, winter – a time of dark and cold – would have been seen as the time when the old year 'died' and the spirits of the dead walked abroad. The festival of *Samhain* was held in October/November (still celebrated today as Halloween), when stock was taken of herds and supplies, and decisions made as to which animals would be slaughtered in order to survive the winter. Tradition suggests it was celebrated by bonfires (to dispel the dark of winter) and communal feasting on the newly harvested food and sacrificed animals – which would fit in well with the evidence from Hallaton. *Imbolc* was another festival marking the start of spring (around February), associated with the goddess Brighid, and was a celebration of the lengthening days and the early signs of spring. *Beltane* took place at the start of the summer pastoral season (April/May) and *Lughanasadh* was a two week long summer festival held at the end of July.

Above: Artist's impression of a druid with flowing white robes, holding a sprig of mistletoe. Drawing by Mike Codd, © Jill Bourne.

We don't know which Gods were worshipped at Hallaton or exactly what the people were asking for in return for their gifts and sacrifices. What we do know is that although the shrine was probably in use from the 1st century BC, the main activities (including the burying of the coins, helmets and pigs) all took place in the years surrounding the Roman invasion. Had rumours that foreign invaders were landing on southern coasts reached Leicestershire, causing the local people to ask their gods for extra protection? Regardless of whether the Corieltavi were anti- or pro-Roman, it was likely to have been a time of great uncertainty; Hallaton also lay close to the border of the Catuvellauni who had already taken over the Trinovantes. It was certainly a time when the protection of the gods was needed on a regular basis.

In today's materialistic world, the burying of valuable objects to gain a god's favour may seem odd, but how many of us still throw coins into wells for good luck?

Gifts to the gods

Hoards of precious objects, coins and weapons are common throughout the prehistoric world, but why did our ancestors bury so much metal in the ground and in rivers and boggy areas? There are many possible reasons, one of the most commonly cited being the fear of having wealth stolen in times of unrest. A famous, much more recent example of this is recorded in Samuel Pepys' diary entry for 13 June 1667, where he asks his wife to bury the family's wealth in their garden in Northamptonshire in advance of possible attacks by the Dutch. He also describes burying wine and cheese to keep it safe during the Great Fire of London.

Archaeologists are often accused of retreating to the term 'ritual' when they don't fully understand the reasons behind archaeological deposits. However, where patterns emerge of objects being deliberately selected and placed in specific, often very visible locations in the landscape over a period of time, such as the late Iron Age torcs from Snettisham or the coins and objects at Hallaton, it seems unlikely that this is anything but ritual activity. Roman ritual deposits are easier to identify as they are usually found in places that have obvious religious significance, such as wells or temples. However, there seems to be a tradition in Britain of burying metal objects as offerings to the gods dating back to the Bronze Age, when hoards of bronze objects such as axe heads were hidden in watery places, and this practice continues into the Iron Age. In fact Bronze Age objects often turn up in Iron Age hoards. Bronze Age spearheads were found close to the hoards at Hallaton.

Of course, the shrine occupied only a small part of the hilltop. If people from distant places gathered there on an annual basis to meet with fellow tribal families and groups, they would probably have taken the opportunity for other activities. Marriage and other alliances, the succession of leaders, trade agreements and coming of age celebrations might all have been carried out under the watchful eye of the gods.

Image © Leicester City Council.

55

People of the Corieltavi

The Corieltavi were the most northerly British people to have produced coins in the Iron Age, but they were relatively obscure compared to some of the other tribes. It was generally assumed that they existed on the periphery between the north of England, Wales and the south-west, where coins were not made, and the more prosperous south-east, where the Catuvellauni (north of the Thames) and the Atrebates (in Berkshire and Hampshire) had important contacts with the Continent. The presence of Roman coins and objects at Hallaton suggests that the Corieltavi, a federation of smaller groups, were more important than previously thought, with their own links to Gaul and the Roman world.

The earliest coins at Hallaton had no inscriptions but writing soon began to appear on them; it would seem that having your name on a coin was an important symbol of power. The Corieltavi began to inscribe their coins in the first half of the 1st century AD. The lettering found on many of the Hallaton coins is among the earliest examples of British writing.

Although we cannot be certain who ordered the minting of the coins and determined what imagery and names went on them, it seems likely that they were chieftains or important people and the inscriptions may be their names. They must have been people with considerable power and wealth, able to control the minting of coins within their territory, and who were familiar with developments in the Roman world.

The use of horse images on most of the Hallaton coins suggests a unifying design or some underlying sense of common identity. However, in a society split into small groups, each with their own leaders, inscriptions would have added importance and meaning to the symbolism on the coins. Having your name on a coin would be a powerful message to your followers and other leaders, and of course it would ensure that the gods knew whom to reward for their gifts.

The first writing

It is likely that the British people would have spoken various Celtic languages but there is no written evidence for these. Writing on coins using the Latin alphabet started to appear in the 1st century BC. Of course the Roman language would have been completely foreign to the native Britons and there is evidence that many did not understand the inscriptions. The die engravers would have originally copied the letters from Roman coins, but the letters on some coins are upside down or backwards suggesting that the inscribers were simply copying shapes without really understanding the meaning of the words. Having an inscription on a coin was probably enough to convey status without it having to be legible.

The original legends on some of the coins have become unrecognisable as letters, and in some cases have simply become part of the pattern.

Do the inscriptions on the coins represent the earliest named British leaders? Those common on the Corieltavian coins include:
VOLISIOS DUMNOCOVEROS, IISVPRASV, TATISOM, AVN COST and VEP CORF
Are these the first known names of Britons from the East Midlands?

The Romans at Hallaton

Although activity on the shrine itself seems to end after the AD 60s, the Romans moved into the area in the later 1st century AD, constructing villages, villas and roads during over 300 years of occupation. A settlement with several roundhouses in a ditched enclosure was established just to the north of the shrine. Pottery from excavations there suggests that these were occupied from the 1st century AD onwards but in contrast to the shrine, this settlement is definitely domestic in nature. Several of the ditches and pits around the shrine, identified by the geophysical survey were excavated. These all contained Roman pottery and other objects and confirmed that people lived on the hilltop throughout the Roman period.

Early Roman contact?

Several of the Hallaton coin hoards contained early Roman coins called *denarii*. Many of these were issued in Republican times and were already over 100 years old when they were buried; many of them were very worn. This is in contrast to the Iron Age coins, which look freshly minted. Roman coins are likely to have been circulating in Britain for some time before the Roman conquest in AD 43, as a result of trading and diplomacy. Contact with the Roman world is well known in the south of Britain, but the presence of so many *denarii* at Hallaton suggests that there was also contact between Leicestershire and Rome before the invasion.

Right: This Roman denarius of Augustus is dated between 2 BC and AD 14 and is in mint condition. Coin shown at 200%. ©Leicestershire County Council.

As well as the silver *denarii* buried with the Iron Age hoards, other Roman coins were also found in some of the later features. These might have been casual losses from the people living on the site or could have been part of religious ceremonies, which perhaps continued the ritual depositions first carried out in the shrine.

A small hoard was found amongst the animal bone deposits. This contained six 2nd- to 3rd-century AD coins, a Roman gold necklace clasp and a Gallo-Belgic coin. The Roman coins and jewellery date the hoard to the 3rd century AD or later, so the Gallo-Belgic coin was over 300 years old when it was buried. Perhaps a Roman found the Iron Age coin and combined it with his own treasures to create a personal offering to the gods, knowing that the hilltop had previously been used for offerings. A descendant of the original Iron Age natives who built the site, despite being Romanised with a new set of deities, may have buried this hoard in return for favours from the old gods. Whatever happened it is clear that some 200 years after the shrine went out of use, the people living there still knew of its existence and what it had originally been used for.

One of Britain's oldest coins?

One of the Republican silver *denarii* from Hallaton could have been made as far back as 211 BC, which would make it one of the oldest Roman coins found in Britain. The presence of this coin is thought to be strong evidence for the exchange of objects between Leicestershire and Rome through trade and diplomacy before the Roman conquest.

Left: This Republican coin was struck in Rome just before the Roman general Scipio defeated Hannibal. It shows the goddess Roma on one side and the twins Castor and Pollux on galloping horses on the reverse. Coin shown at 150%. © Leicestershire County Council.

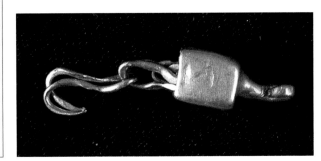

Left: This 25mm long gold clasp from a necklace or bracelet was left on the site as an offering 200 years after the shrine had supposedly gone out of use. © Leicestershire County Council.

The sacred hilltop

It likely that the Roman inhabitants knew of the importance of the hilltop prior to building their houses there. The site would have been a particularly good location for a settlement, on the crest of a hill, close to other Roman settlements including the small town at Medbourne, and served by several Roman roads. Interestingly, despite the evidence for Roman activity here, the actual ritual area was very carefully left undisturbed. Did the Romans know what the shrine meant to the previous inhabitants and choose to leave it alone despite its prime position on the ridge? Perhaps they feared that desecrating a sacred site would anger the native gods. The complete lack of Roman features or artefacts suggests that the shrine itself was taboo and remained so for the better part of 300 years.

Roman finds from both metal detecting and the excavations include coins, jewellery and other objects. This amount of metalwork is unusual for a typical Romano-British settlement and some items seem to have been deliberately damaged. In particular many of the 1st–2nd century AD brooches may have had their pins deliberately ripped off – possibly to ritually 'kill' the objects and render them useless in their current life and presumably make them more acceptable to the gods. It appears that the ritual nature of the site continued after the Iron Age shrine was abandoned by the native people and that the Romans continued to use the hilltop for their own religious and ritual ceremonies, perhaps believing the hill to be particularly close to the gods. Although only a few Roman features were dug, finds of tile, brick, rubble and tesserae (small tiles used to make mosaics) suggest that there were definitely buildings nearby. The Romans might well have incorporated a temple into their settlement close to the old shrine.

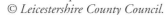

Left: These two objects are similar to sceptre handles and terminals found on several Roman temple sites. Over forty similar examples were found at Wanborough (Surrey), along with other religious regalia such as head-dresses. They are thought to be 2nd-century AD in date.
© Leicestershire County Council.

Below: This 56mm long curved copper alloy object is part of the wing of a metal oil lamp (left) probably dating to the 1st century AD. Metal lamps are rare in Roman Britain but might have been used in a temple.
© Leicestershire County Council.

Roman offerings?

One feature that could indicate that the Roman inhabitants were carrying out ritual ceremonies was a small pit dug into the hillside, just south of the shrine deposits. The pit was over 1.2m deep and had been excavated into the water table with waterlogged deposits at the very base. As well as hundreds of sherds of Roman pottery, the objects found included a broken Roman copper armlet (*below right*), again possibly deliberately damaged, several 4th-century minims (tiny Roman coins), hobnails and copper alloy fragments. The tip of a Bronze Age spear was also found in the pit (*below left*). Prehistoric objects are often found on later ritual sites and it is thought that Roman 'archaeologists' on finding such an object recognised it as ancient and incorporated it in their own ritual deposits.

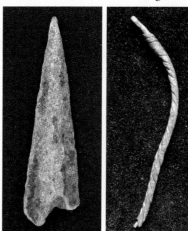

Spear, length 68mm.
Bracelet, length 73mm.

Photographs © Leicestershire County Council.

Links to the Present

Why Hallaton?

Today Hallaton is a small village not far from Market Harborough; pretty enough with its impressive church, thatched buildings and the old butter cross on the green, but not exceptionally remarkable. There is certainly nothing to suggest that 2000 years ago this area was a communal meeting place for large groups of Iron Age people. However one unusual event occurs in the village every Easter Monday: a strange ritual is enacted, when villagers from Hallaton and Medbourne play host to one of the oldest surviving and most bizarre customs of rural England – the Hallaton Bottle Kicking and Hare Pie Scramble. Hare pie and penny loaves are distributed outside the church in the morning, and the bottle kicking takes place in the afternoon from a spot above the village known as 'Hare Pie Bank'.

Although the origins of this strange ritual are unknown, it is reported in a letter written by John Tailby in 1796, where it was described as an 'ancient custom'. More recently documentary evidence has uncovered the existence of the previously unknown Saint Morell and suggests that his chapel stood on Hare Pie Bank and may well be linked with the custom. The will of a Hallaton priest dated 1532 requesting his curate to go on pilgrimage to four shrines, one of them 'St Mawrell of Hallaton', suggests that this could have been an important place for both worship and pilgrimage in medieval times. The village church of St Michael is large for the size of the village and once had a great charnel house and two towers, one of which may have been used as an external pulpit to preach to masses of people who came on pilgrimage. Exactly how far back the cult of St Morell goes is unknown but he is believed to have re-dedicated Pagan shrines. Between 2011–2013 geophysical survey and excavations by ULAS and the HFWG have found Roman features and the remains of a medieval chapel and cemetery on Hare Pie Bank.

Although there are no firm links between the Hallaton shrine, St Morell's chapel and the bottle kicking custom, it would not be unusual for the later generations to choose a location for their religious buildings or customs in a place already known to be 'sacred'. We know from the excavations that the Romans were active on Hare Pie Bank and it is possible that the followers of St Morell located their chapel there because of the special significance of the area. The original bottle kickers may have adopted the location of a local cult to sanctify their activities. Further excavations are planned on top of the hill and it is hoped that more evidence will be found to link today's strange practices back to the Iron Age people and their offerings of coins metalwork and pigs.

The legend

The Hare Pie legend tells that two ladies of Hallaton were saved from a raging bull by a hare that distracted the animal. In gratitude the ladies donated money to the church to provide hare pie, twelve penny-loaves and two barrels of beer for the poor of the village every Easter Monday.

Top: Villager John Morison (the Warrener) leads the procession through the village holding aloft a bronze statue of a hare with baskets of penny loaves and Hare Pie. Outside the church gate the pie is blessed and the bread and pie distributed to the waiting crowd by flinging them through the air.

Bottom: The Bottle kicking starts at Hare Pie Bank above the village. The 'bottles' are three small casks (two filled with ale and a dummy) each weighing 5kg. The players represent Hallaton and its neighbouring village of Medbourne and the objective is to get the 'bottle' across the stream nearest to each village. The bottle is thrown in the air at the start and then it's a mad scrum to wrestle the bottle across the goal. The winning village is decided by the best of three bottles, but that is really the only rule.
Photographs © Chris Clarke.

St Morell's Chapel – A Medieval Shrine?

Recent work by the HFWG may have uncovered a link between the 2000 year old shrine and the modern bottle kicking tradition. Over the last few years fieldwork on Hare Pie Bank, the traditional starting point for the bottle kicking, have uncovered the remains of a lost chapel dedicated to the obscure Saint Morell, which is thought to have been a place of pilgrimage.

The site was first identified in 2006 when a small area of the bank was surveyed using resistivity (which shows up features with higher or lower resistance than their surroundings) at the end of a very dry spell of weather. The initial results showed a square feature and the group began discussing what it might be. It didn't look particularly church-like and a possible resemblance to a Roman temple had locals and archaeologists alike arguing about its date and function. However, over the next few years attempts to replicate the survey failed miserably, and the group concluded that the very dry conditions must have enhanced the results.

Finally, dry weather in the first half of 2011 inspired the HFWG to try again, this time successfully, and a much clearer picture emerged. A square enclosure (approximately 36 metres across) was revealed, with internal features and a straight line running north-east to south-west. The group realised that the only way to determine whether these features could be those mentioned by Tailby in the 18th century – 'a small oblong bank, 10 yards long and 6 wide; with a small olde trench around it, and a circular hole in the centre' – and thought to be the remnants of St Morell's chapel, was to excavate. Once again the HFWG joined forces with ULAS and, with the help of Julian and Sarah White, the landowners, planned a community excavation.

In the first season in 2011, three small hand-dug trenches suggested that the square enclosure was the remnants of a bank, probably medieval in date with Roman features beneath it. Tantalisingly, although no building was found, wall plaster, tile and stone were recovered, which hinted at a demolished building nearby. Several fragments of human bone were also recovered. Spurred on by these results the group spent the winter raising money with coffee mornings, talks and car boot sales and, helped by a grant from the Leicestershire Archaeological and Historical Society, a larger excavation was carried out in 2012.

The raised area on Hare Pie Bank was an artificial platform of made-ground created by over 1m of demolition rubble and debris including stone, tile and plaster. Once the rubble was removed the outline of the building that once stood there was revealed.

Above right: HFWG members cleaning the robber trench of the building wall. The raised area shows the remnants of the plaster floor inside the chapel.

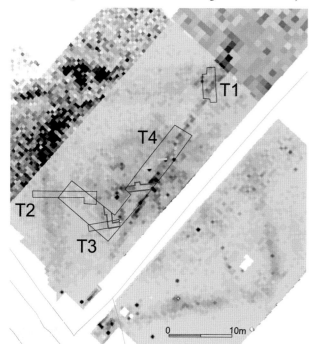

Left: The group used a combination of magnetometry and resistivity at very close intervals to get as clear a picture as possible. The result shows internal features inside a square enclosure. The line running north-east to south-west is a modern trackway. Trenches 1 and 2 revealed the remains of a bank, while Trench 4 found the vestiges of the chapel buried beneath rubble from its demolition. The red lines show the walls of the chapel and the burials are marked in green.

None of the walls had survived but the 'robber trenches' (the rubble-filled ditches that remained after people had dug out the stone foundations to re-use elsewhere) were clearly visible. In the centre of the building a plaster surface with square patterns was uncovered, all that was left of the tiled floor. The HFWG were convinced that they had found the remains of St Morell's chapel where people might once have flocked on pilgrimage.

Outside the building however, the excavations uncovered something rather more disturbing. Five burials were revealed – not particularly unusual in the context of a chapel – but these skeletons displayed some unusual features. All were aligned with their head to the west in the Christian tradition. One was a small child placed on their side. Another had been laid to rest in an elongated pit in an unusual position that looked almost as if they had been flung in on their back. Close by, an upright skull and fragments of a hand suggested another burial within a band of rubble. The only burial found to the west of the chapel had a strange triangular hole in the top of the head. The lack of fractures around the hole suggests that this was not caused by damage after burial, but was perhaps something more sinister. It could perhaps represent some kind of medical surgery, but the most likely explanation is that it was caused by a blow to the head with a sharp weapon. The head and shoulders of a fifth skeleton had been disturbed by a modern water pipe.

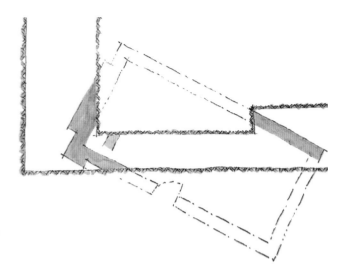

Radiocarbon determinations on two of the skeletons place the burials in the 14th century, which is consistent with the pottery recovered. Several medieval pennies were also found dating from the 13th–15th centuries. Could these have been deliberately left behind by medieval pilgrims seeking healing or favours from the saint?

The reasons behind the strange collection of bodies remain a mystery. Was burial at the chapel (rather than the church in Hallaton) reserved for a particular group of people, perhaps criminals or people with a particular illness? Whatever the reason, the siting of the start of the bottle kicking on the exact location of the chapel suggests that a tradition that harks back to the earlier use of the place.

Roman features and finds were also recorded in the excavations, and with the presence of the Iron Age shrine just a few hundred metres away, the Hallaton bottle kicking tradition could actually be the culmination of over 2000 years of tradition and ritual here!

Above: Sketch showing the possible layout of the chapel, by Anthony Goode (HFWG).

Left: Some of the unusual burials associated with the chapel included a skeleton positioned on its back, one with a triangular hole in the forehead and a skull buried upright in a band of rubble.

Acknowledgements

First and foremost thanks must go to the Hallaton Field Work Group (HFWG) and their friends and families, particularly Ken and Hazel Wallace, who made the initial find and whose enthusiasm and dedication made it possible for the site to be properly investigated and the story of the treasure to be told. Thanks also to the landowners, Mr and Mrs David Higgs, and the tenant farmer, Mr Michael Higgs, for allowing the investigations to take place. Too many people participated in the excavations to name them all here but grateful thanks are extended to everyone in ULAS, HFWG, The School of Archaeology and Ancient History, Leicestershire County Council and anyone else who gave their time and help.

Specialist help and advice was provided by numerous bodies including Ian Leins (Iron Age and Roman coins) and Marilyn Hockey (conservation) and their colleagues at the British Museum, Alex Brogden at the Goldsmiths' Company, John Morison and Graham Jones who supplied insights into the local history of Hallaton and St Morrell, staff at Harborough Museum, Market Harborough and Leicestershire County Council, in particular Helen Sharp and Pete Liddle, and also Carol Kirby at Hallaton Museum. Expert advice was also provided by Colin Haselgrove, Simon James, Jeremy Taylor, Graham Morgan and Julia Farley of the School of Archaeology and Ancient History, University of Leicester and ULAS colleagues, particularly Jen Browning (animal bone), Elizabeth Johnson (prehistoric and Roman pottery), Nick Cooper (pottery and small finds), Angela Monckton and Anita Radini (environmental data), Debbie Sawday (post-Roman pottery), Lynden Cooper (lithics). Thanks also to Adrian Butler (geophysics) and Derek Hamilton (radiocarbon dating).

The project was funded from numerous sources, notably English Heritage, the British Museum, the BBC and the Roman Research Trust. The post-excavation and publication work was supported by English Heritage, the Society of Antiquaries of London, Leicestershire Archaeological and Historical Society, HFWG and University of Leicester Archaeological Services (ULAS). The Heritage Lottery Fund provided a grant for the display of materials in Harborough Museum, which included a contribution towards the conservation. The College of Arts, Humanities and Law, University of Leicester provided a grant towards the cost of this publication.

Thanks are also due to Leicestershire County Council, which now owns the treasure, for allowing use of their reconstruction images and photographs. Images were also provided by Leicestershire County Council, the British Museum, The Collection: Art and Archaeology in Lincolnshire, Winchester City Council Museums Service, Dave Hopkins, Mike Codd, Jill Bourne, ULAS staff and HFWG members including Chris Clarke, Anthony Goode and the late Chris Royall.

We are grateful to Patrick Clay, Richard Buckley, Pam Lowther, Debbie Sawday, Jennifer Browning and other ULAS colleagues for their comments on the text. The author takes full responsibility for any errors and omissions.

Some of the Hallaton Field Work Group stalwarts in 2003 after backfilling the site. From left to right: Carol Kirby, Tony Payne, Chrissie Brammall, Sue Horsley, Ken Wallace, Chris Royall. Front: Hazel Wallace, Jon Cracknell.

Interested in More?

Harborough Museum and Market Harborough Library

The Hallaton Treasure Gallery within the museum and library in Market Harborough showcases the key finds alongside interactive and informative displays. Re-opening Spring 2014.

Address: The Symington Building, Adam and Eve Street,
Market Harborough LE16 7AG
Telephone: 0116 305 3627
Email: harboroughmuseum@leics.gov.uk
Web: www.leics.gov.uk/harboroughmuseum/treasure

Hallaton Museum

The small museum in Hallaton has an impressive display based around the finding of the treasure.
Open weekends and Bank Holidays Easter – end of September.

Address: The Tin Tab, Churchgate, Hallaton, Leicestershire, LE16 8TY
Email: grapaul@talktalk.net (Pauline Ingham)
Web: www.leicestershirevillages.com/hallaton/hallatonmuseum.html

Leicestershire County Council Museums

Leicestershire County Council Museum Service curates the collection of objects known as the Hallaton Treasure. Finds not on public display are accessible by appointment.

Email: archaeology@leics.gov.uk
Web: www.leics.gov.uk/archaeology

Leicestershire Fieldworkers

Leicestershire Fieldworkers has, since 1976, undertaken through its local groups, an award-winning programme of archaeological fieldwork throughout Leicestershire, Leicester and Rutland. The group, in conjunction with Leicestershire County Council Museums Service archaeologists, holds regular lecture meetings, has its own newsletter, *The Fieldworker*, and provides training courses for beginners.

Contact: Fieldworker Enquiries, 37 Church Road, Nailstone, CV13 0QH
Email: info@leicsfieldworkers.co.uk
Web: www.leicsfieldworkers.co.uk

Hallaton Field Work Group

The HFWG is one of the many Leicestershire Fieldworkers local groups set up to find out more about the heritage of east Leicestershire. This active group undertakes fieldwalking as well as geophysical survey using equipment purchased with a grant from the Lottery Heritage Fund in Hallaton and the surrounding areas. They also give talks and training sessions and run annual excavations. The group often lends their expertise to other groups and also works in conjunction with University of Leicester, ULAS and the County Council.

Contact: Ce Ponting
Telephone: 01858 545452
Email: hallatonfwg@yahoo.co.uk
Web: http://www.leicestershirevillages.com/hallaton/fieldworking-group.html

Portable Antiquities Scheme

If you think you have found an archaeological object you can find out more about what to do and how to contact your local Finds Liaison Officer at **www.finds.org.uk**

Leicestershire: Wendy Scott
Telephone: 0116 3058325
Email: wendy.scott@leics.gov.uk

Northamptonshire: Julie Cassidy
Telephone: 01604 367249
Email: juCassidy@northamptonshire.gov.uk